**Royal
Geographical
Society**
with IBG

Advancing geography
and geographical learning

# THE
# EXPLORATION
## TREASURY

Rolex's long association with the Society dates from the 1930s and was celebrated in the first summiting of Everest in 1953. Today, Rolex supports the Society's unique photographic holdings and the wider care and conservation of its internationally important Collections relating to the history of exploration and travel.

**Royal Geographical Society**
with IBG

Advancing geography
and geographical learning

Founded in 1830, the Royal Geographical Society (with IBG) is dedicated to the development and promotion of geographical knowledge, together with its application to the challenges facing society and the environment. For more information on the Society's contemporary work please visit: www.rgs.org

This is an André Deutsch book

Published in 2017 by André Deutsch Limited
A division of the Carlton Publishing Group
20 Mortimer Street
London W1T 3JW

Text © Beau Riffenburgh, 2017
Design © Carlton Books Limited, 2017

A catalogue record for this book is available from the British Library.

ISBN: 978 0 233 00475 4

10 9 8 7 6 5 4 3 2 1

Printed in China.

Publishing credits:
Picture research: Jamie Owen
Editor: Alison Moss
Design: Russell Knowles, Katie Baxendale
Production: Sarah Kramer

**COVER IMAGE:** Details from a map showing the exploring journeys led by Robert Falcon Scott during the British National Antarctic Expedition (1901–04) and made during Ernest Shackleton's British Antarctic Expedition (1907–09). Both expeditions included treks from the bases on Ross Island south onto or across the Great Ice Barrier, as well as through the Western Mountains and onto the Polar Plateau. The map was produced primarily to show the route of Shackleton's farthest south.

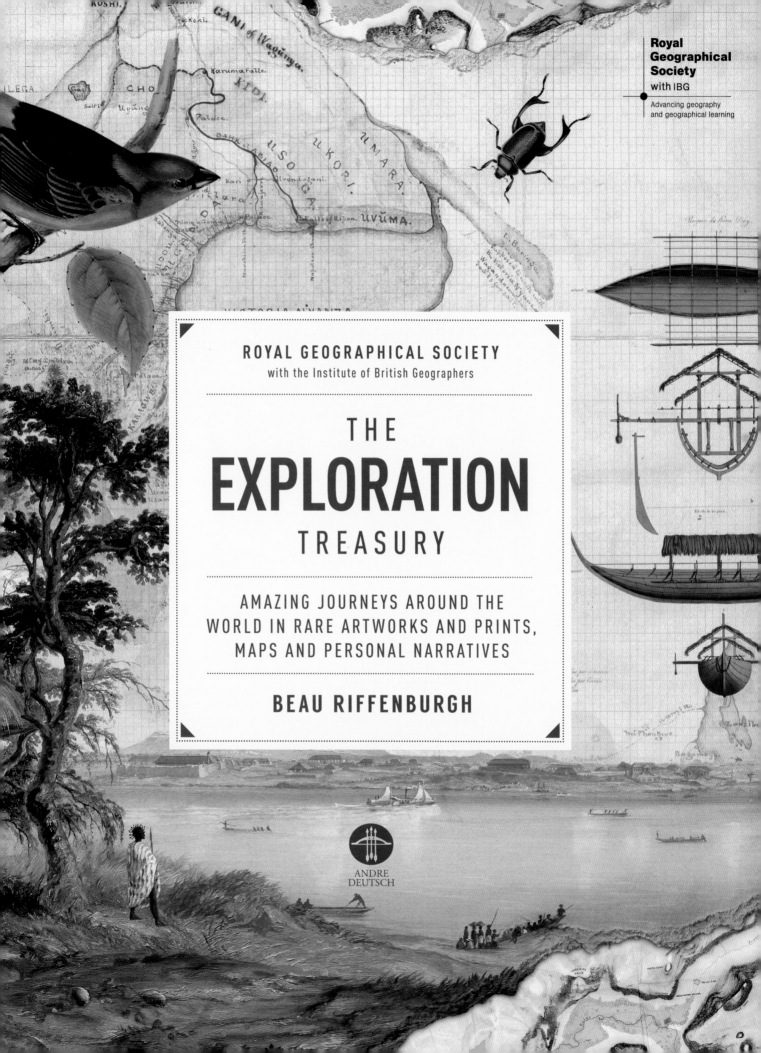

Royal
Geographical
Society
with IBG

Advancing geography
and geographical learning

ROYAL GEOGRAPHICAL SOCIETY
with the Institute of British Geographers

# THE
# EXPLORATION
## TREASURY

AMAZING JOURNEYS AROUND THE
WORLD IN RARE ARTWORKS AND PRINTS,
MAPS AND PERSONAL NARRATIVES

## BEAU RIFFENBURGH

ANDRE
DEUTSCH

In loving memory of my grandparents:
Cecil Dewey Kelley – a professional photographer –
and Gertrude Faith Kelley (née Campbell).

## AUTHOR'S ACKNOWLEDGEMENTS

The images used herein all come from the archives and other holdings of
the Royal Geographical Society (with IBG). This book benefited immeasurably
from the knowledge and expertise of Jamie Owen, the Society's Picture
Library Sales Manager, as well as the vision of Alison Moss of
Carlton Books Ltd.

I also wish to express my thanks to Caroline Curtis, Bill Hamilton of A.M.
Heath & Company, and designer Katie Baxendale for their invaluable
contributions. I am also extremely grateful for the editorial input given
throughout this project by Dr Liz Cruwys.

OPPOSITE: Train crossing a bridge on the railway line between the Peruvian
cities of Lima and La Oroya. The photograph was taken in 1907 by the South
American explorer Lieutenant Colonel Percy H. Fawcett.

# CONTENTS

R. Burton, delt.                    C.F. Kell, Lith.

THE PILGRIM.

# INTRODUCTION

THROUGHOUT MUCH OF THE NINETEENTH CENTURY, MANY EUROPEANS – INCLUDING POLITICIANS, INDUSTRIALISTS, ADMINISTRATORS, EDUCATORS, AND MILITARY OFFICERS – AGREED THAT GEOGRAPHICAL KNOWLEDGE WAS THE KEY TO IMPERIAL POWER. "THE ATTEMPT TO BUILD AN EMPIRE OR TO DEVELOP ITS RESOURCES WITHOUT GEOGRAPHY," SAID DOUGLAS W. FRESHFIELD, PRESIDENT OF THE ROYAL GEOGRAPHICAL SOCIETY (RGS), "IS LIKE BUILDING A HOUSE WITHOUT FIRST CONSIDERING THE CLIMATE OR THE LOCALITY, OR SEEING THE CHARACTER OF THE SOIL ON WHICH YOU MUST PLANT ITS FOUNDATIONS."

Knowledge, as Sir John Barrow – "the father of British exploration" – asserted many times, was power, and exploration produced geographical knowledge. And so Barrow was involved in virtually every significant British exploring expedition for the 40 years that he served as the Second Secretary to the Admiralty. Exploration produced the geographical knowledge necessary for the military strategies, administrative incorporation, economic development, and cultural domination that marked European imperialism.

In its early forms, this knowledge was transmitted by means of maps, coastal charts, and imagery of settlements, people, and the natural world. As colonial empires expanded, the need for information to aid troop movements, imports and exports, and tax collection saw the development of trigonometric surveys and means by which to chart river systems, map hidden passes, and delineate political boundaries.

Thus, for some two centuries, European imperialism and its necessary antecedent, exploration, were inviolably bound with

**OPPOSITE**: Self portrait by Richard Francis Burton when he was disguised as a Pathan pilgrim in order to surreptitiously reach Mecca in 1853.

**BELOW**: The citadel and fort of Kala Fath in Afghanistan, sketched by Thomas Hungerford Holdich, who was president of the RGS in 1917–19.

geography – and science and technology – as they were all attempts to understand, conquer, and control the world. The exploration of the Pacific by James Cook, for example, was a perfect marriage of imperial expansion and scientific and geographical investigation.

For most of the British imperial period, geography and exploration were linked via an institutional base that was also closely tied to the government's expansionist ambitions. Geographers provided both the practical information necessary for such expansion and the intellectual justification for it.

At the close of the eighteenth century and the opening years of the nineteenth, this institutional body was the African Association, which, under the leadership of Sir Joseph Banks, sponsored African explorers such as John Ledyard and Mungo Park. Banks' position as the foremost promoter of exploration eventually passed to Barrow, who was behind the ventures of Hugh Clapperton and Richard Lander to West Africa, and Arctic expeditions led by John Ross, William Edward Parry, and John Franklin.

In 1827, Barrow became a founding member of the Raleigh Club – a dining society of travellers who among them had visited nearly every known part of the Earth. Three years later, Barrow chaired a club meeting in which it was decided to establish a society for the advancement of geographical science. In July 1830, the Geographical Society of London was founded, with Viscount Goderich, a former Prime Minister, as its first president, and Barrow and Franklin among its vice-presidents. When King William IV became its patron, the name was changed to the Royal Geographical Society. In the following years, the African Association and the Raleigh Club merged into the RGS.

In the next century, the RGS became the largest and one of the most influential geographical societies in the world. Meanwhile, the drive and connections of some of its powerful presidents – such as Barrow, Sir Roderick Murchison, Sir George Goldie,

and Earl Curzon of Kedleston – brought it more closely into the mainstream of imperial expansion. The RGS consolidated its position as Britain's primary geographical institution by promoting and sponsoring scientific exploration, particularly in Africa, Asia, and the polar regions. Under the presidency of Murchison, the Society backed David Livingstone, Richard Francis Burton, John Hanning Speke, and Samuel Baker. Several decades later, another president, Sir Clements Markham, was the key figure in launching Britain's entry into Antarctic exploration, as the man behind the British National Antarctic Expedition, led by Robert Falcon Scott.

The reputation of the RGS grew to such an extent that most explorers – regardless of country of origin or destination – applied to it for recognition, advice, and funding. In return, it became a repository for expedition diaries, correspondence, maps, artefacts, paintings, and photographs. Today, its collections include some two million items covering 500 years of geographical exploration.

This book showcases some of the truly special and beautiful holdings in the Society's collections. The maps, diary passages, paintings, and photographs all were important methods of transferring knowledge about places that most people would never experience. Therefore, those who produced them tended to aspire to a scientific objectivity in their work, which would allow them, as impartial observers, to give completely accurate information. Needless to say, they were not truly objective or neutral, but were driven by cultural preconditions, underlying assumptions, and expectations that helped determine how they saw and recorded people, places, and events.

Yet, in some senses, this makes the written and visual representations even more fascinating today. For those presented in this book shine a light not just on regions or peoples little known to Europeans, or on the general geographical knowledge gathered by these explorers, but on the explorers themselves and the beliefs, values, and expectations of their own society and time.

**OPPOSITE**: The court of a Buddhist temple in Kathmandu, painted in water colours by Dr Henry Ambrose Oldfield, who served as the surgeon to the British Residency in Nepal from 1850 to 1863.

**ABOVE**: The rapids of of the Rio Negro near São Gabriel da Cachoeira in Brazil. Drawn by Charles Bentley, the view was first sketched during the RGS expedition to British Guiana, led by Robert H. Schomburgk.

BEAU RIFFENBURGH

Pl XXVIII.

*Simia trivirgata.*

Huet, fils, d'après une esquisse de Mr. de Humboldt.     De l'Imprimerie de Langlois.     Bouquet sculpsit.

# ALEXANDER VON HUMBOLDT

## EXPEDITION TO THE AMERICAS, 1799–1804

FRIEDRICH WILHELM HEINRICH ALEXANDER VON HUMBOLDT (1769–1859) WAS CLEARLY ONE OF THE GREATEST INTELLECTS AND NATURAL HISTORIANS OF ALL TIME. BORN IN BERLIN, HE WAS FASCINATED BY BOTANY FROM A YOUNG AGE. HE ATTENDED THE UNIVERSITY OF GÖTTINGEN, WHERE HE MET GEORG FORSTER, WHO HAD BEEN THE BOTANICAL DRAUGHTSMAN ON JAMES COOK'S SECOND VOYAGE.

They travelled to England together, where Humboldt came to know the famed botanist Sir Joseph Banks. Both Banks and Forster undoubtedly influenced Humboldt's decision to spend his life as a gentleman traveller and scientist.

In 1792, Humboldt was appointed an inspector in the Prussian Department of Mines, but he continued to spend his spare time investigating the plant life of Freiberg and other local areas. When his mother died four years later, leaving him a substantial inheritance, he resigned to pursue his travel interests. In Paris he happened to meet the French botanist Aimé Bonpland, and the two travelled together to Spain. There, with the backing of the minister from Saxony and the Spanish foreign minister, they were presented to King Charles IV, who approved their plan to visit – at their own expense – the regions of the Americas under Spanish rule. There they could study and investigate whatever they wished on condition they reported back on the status of the mineral deposits throughout the domains.

Taking with them many scientific instruments, Humboldt and Bonpland arrived at Cumaná in Venezuela in July 1799, and were immediately entranced by the wealth of plant and animal life. After several months of recording many species with which they were previously unfamiliar, they sailed down the coast in an open boat, then moved on to Caracas. In February 1800 they began a wandering trek throughout the little-known interior, hoping to determine the relationship between the Amazon and

**OPPOSITE**: A three-striped night monkey (or owl monkey). From the rain forests of Venezuela and north-central Brazil, they feed on fruit, nuts, leaves, and insects. Humboldt's classification of *Simia trivirgata* was changed to *Aotus trivirgatus* after chromosomal research. The illustration is from an original sketch by Humboldt.

**BELOW**: A brown-mantled tamarind, one of many squirrel-sized New World monkeys. Found in northwestern South America, they are today classified as *Saguinus fuscicollis*, although Humboldt named them *Simia leonina*.

VULTUR GRYPHUS Lin.

RECUEIL

D'OBSERVATIONS DE ZOOLOGIE

ET D'ANATOMIE COMPARÉE,

FAITES

DANS L'OCÉAN ATLANTIQUE, DANS L'INTÉRIEUR DU NOUVEAU CONTINENT ET DANS LA MER
DU SUD PENDANT LES ANNÉES 1799, 1800, 1801, 1802 et 1803;

PAR AL. DE HUMBOLDT ET A. BONPLAND.

PREMIER VOLUME.

A PARIS,

Chez F. SCHOELL, LIBRAIRE, RUE DES FOSSÉS-MONTMARTRE, N.º 14.
Et chez G.ᵐᵉ DUFOUR et COMP.ᵗᵉ, RUE DES MATHURINS-SAINT-JACQUES, N.º 7.

1811.

Orinoco rivers. They travelled partly by water and partly through the jungle and then crossed the *llanos* – barren, hot, waterless plains. At one point, they discovered electric eels, which they captured and dissected despite receiving unpleasant shocks throughout the process.

Once they reached the Orinoco, they travelled south, tormented by insects, surviving encounters with crocodiles and jaguars, portaging their canoes around cataracts, capsizing more than once, and running out of food. Even so, they managed to map much of the watershed between the Orinoco and the Amazon, as well as to compile remarkable natural history collections.

In November 1800, after recovering from malaria and typhoid, Humboldt and Bonpland sailed to Havana. Three months later they returned to the mainland at Cartagena, from where they charted the Rio Magdalena and continued to Bogotá by mule. A four-month journey then took them to Quito, from where they attempted to climb Mount Chimborazo. They reached an altitude of about 18,400 feet (5,610 m) – a record that would stand for 30 years. Afterwards, they headed south, descending to Trujillo in the coastal desert. Near there, Humboldt was the first to observe and study the cold, low-salinity ocean current later named after him.

In October 1802, still going south, they arrived at Lima and then Callao, where they observed a transit of Mercury. They then sailed north to Guayaquil, made an excursion into the nearby forests, and sailed on to Panama and then Acapulco. For the next year the

two men lived in Mexico City, where Humboldt wrote his classic *History of New Spain*.

In March 1804, they again sailed to Havana, from where Bonpland returned to Europe. Humboldt, however, went north to the United States, where he was hosted by President Thomas Jefferson. Humboldt left Philadelphia for France in July 1804, taking with him thousands of plant, animal and rock specimens; hundreds of maps and drawings; and a rich collection of observations about the indigenous and European inhabitants of Latin America.

For the next three decades, while receiving innumerable honours from learned societies, Humboldt worked on the 30-volume account of his travels, *Le voyage aux régions equinoxiales du Noveau Continent*. This and his many other works inspired some of the great thinkers of the nineteenth century, including Charles Darwin, John Muir, Henry David Thoreau, George Perkins Marsh, and the brothers Richard and Robert Schomburgk.

**ABOVE LEFT:** An Andean condor, one of the largest birds in the world, with a wingspan up to 10 feet 10 inches (3.3 m).

**ABOVE RIGHT:** The title page of Humboldt and Bonpland's work on the zoological and comparative anatomical observations made during their years in South America. The featured illustrations all come from this volume.

**OPPOSITE:** A variety of beetles illustrated by Humboldt. Beetles form the order Coleoptera, which constitutes almost a quarter of all known life forms.

*Pl. XV.*

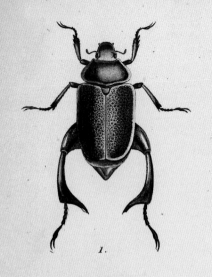

1.

2.

3.

4.

5.

6.

7.

8.

10.

11.

12.

9.

**COUSCOUS BLANC MÂLE.** (Cuscus albus, N.)

Kapoune des naturels du Port-Praslin.

*NOUV. IRLANDE.*

Prêtre pinx.

De l'imp.ⁱᵉ de Rémond.

Coutant sculp.

# CIRCUMNAVIGATIONS

## LOUIS-CLAUDE DE FREYCINET, 1817–20; LOUIS-ISIDORE DUPERREY, 1822–25

WHEN LOUIS-CLAUDE DE FREYCINET (1779–1841) DREW UP PLANS FOR A VOYAGE AROUND THE WORLD IN 1816, IT SEEMED THAT FEW, IF ANY, MARINERS IN FRANCE WERE AS WELL QUALIFIED. HE HAD BEEN A JUNIOR OFFICER WHO WAS PROMOTED DURING THE 1800–03 EXPEDITION LED BY NICOLAS BAUDIN, WHICH HAD EXPLORED MUCH OF THE AUSTRALIAN COAST AND FAMOUSLY ENCOUNTERED THE BRITISH NAVIGATOR MATTHEW FLINDERS.

Baudin died before the end of the expedition, so another officer, François Peron, began the task of writing the official expedition account. When he, too, died, Freycinet took over the task. He then proceeded to denigrate the contributions of Baudin, ignore the discoveries of Flinders, and give as much credit as possible to himself.

As a result of this self-aggrandizing, Freycinet was appointed to lead a new expedition. His instructions were to concentrate on broad scientific work rather than geographical discoveries. However, the independent-minded scientists under Baudin had caused various problems, so Freycinet decided instead to take naval officers with some scientific background.

The ship *Uranie* sailed from Toulon in September 1817 with Freycinet's wife smuggled aboard and secreted in the captain's cabin. Presented to the officers and men – wearing male clothing – she was soon accepted. After stopping at Rio de Janeiro, the ship re-crossed the Atlantic to Cape Town, and thence proceeded to Mauritius – the former Ile de France, which had recently come under British control. There, in May 1818, while *Uranie* was refitted, Freycinet met his brother, whom he had not seen in 15 years.

The expedition made excellent time across the Indian Ocean, reaching the west coast of Australia in September. Freycinet then visited Timor, Ambon and other islands in the Moluccas, and numerous islands along the northwest coast of New Guinea. After passing through the Caroline Islands, they spent 11 weeks at Guam, then sailed to Hawaii, which they reached in August 1819. From there, Freycinet turned south again, and in September *Uranie* anchored in Port Jackson in New South Wales. For a month, botanical and zoological specimens were collected, eventually numbering in the thousands.

Sailing east, *Uranie* passed Campbell Island off the south coast of New Zealand and was sped ahead by heavy winds all the way to

South America. At the beginning of February they safely rounded Cape Horn, and, as Rose Freycinet wrote, "we were at last sailing in the ocean which washes the shores of France, and we thought that we were already home." However, hoping to resupply at the Falkland Islands, Freycinet took *Uranie* into a bay there, where she struck a submerged rock. Badly holed, she had to be deliberately run aground before she sank. Many of the natural history samples were lost or damaged.

A month later, *Mercury*, a ship carrying guns for Chilean rebels, was hailed. Her captain agreed to take the French to Rio de

CHEFS DE LA NOUVELLE-ZÉLANDE.

1. Toui      2. Autre chef

**ABOVE:** Maori chiefs that Duperrey met when he landed in New Zealand. Duperrey stayed two weeks in the vicinity of the Bay of Islands and Manawaora Bay along the coast of the North Island.

**OPPOSITE:** A white cuscus, an arboreal and nocturnal marsupial from northern Australia and Papua New Guinea seen on Duperry's voyage. Originally thought to be a monkey, it is closely related to the possum.

Janeiro, but the passengers already aboard objected. Eventually, Freycinet simply purchased the ship, offloaded the existing crew and passengers at Montevideo, and sailed north in the renamed *Physicienne*. The expedition reached Le Havre in November 1820, and a court-martial lasting an hour and a half acquitted Freycinet of responsibility for losing *Uranie*. He was promoted and spent the rest of his life preparing the 15-volume account of the voyage.

A year after the expedition's return, one of Freycinet's lieutenants, Louis-Isidore Duperrey (1786–1865), proposed a follow-up scientific expedition. This was approved with the proviso that he investigate western Australia as a potential site for French convict resettlement; it was not yet recognized as a British territory.

Sailing from Toulon in the corvette *Coquille* in August 1822, the expedition established a temporary observatory near where *Uranie* had been beached in the Falklands. They then rounded Cape Horn into the Pacific. Following the coastline north to Peru, they turned southwest and crossed the ocean to Tahiti, which they reached in May 1823.

For the next five months *Coquille* cruised the South Pacific, visiting Bora Bora, Tonga, Vanikoro, New Ireland, New Guinea and numerous other islands, and finally arriving at Ambon. After six weeks of restocking the ship and conducting scientific studies, Duperrey took *Coquille* to Australia, passing south of Van Diemen's Land (Tasmania) and arriving at Port Jackson in January 1824. During the two months taken for ship repairs, the officers and crew enjoyed an extensive shore leave. As at previous locations where the ship had called, many drawings of local scenes, peoples, and animals were produced.

Upon sailing from Australia, Duperrey visited New Zealand, then sailed west, calling at Rotuma, the Gilbert Islands (now Kiribati), the Marshall Islands and the Caroline Islands. The explorers then headed south to New Guinea and into what is today Indonesia. From there, they made their way back to Ile de Bourbon (now Réunion), Mauritius, St Helena and Ascension Island, finally reaching Marseilles in March 1825.

The expedition was an unqualified success. Not only had it been the first circumnavigation without the loss of a single life, but the 53 maps and charts produced corrected many geographical errors. In addition, 300 rock samples, 1,200 insects, 264 birds and mammals, 63 reptiles, and 288 fish were donated to the Muséum d'Histoire Naturelle, Paris.

Extensive botanical investigations had also been made by the second-in-command, Jules-Sébastien-César Dumont d'Urville. Only two months after the expedition's return, he presented a proposal for a second circumnavigation in *Coquille*.

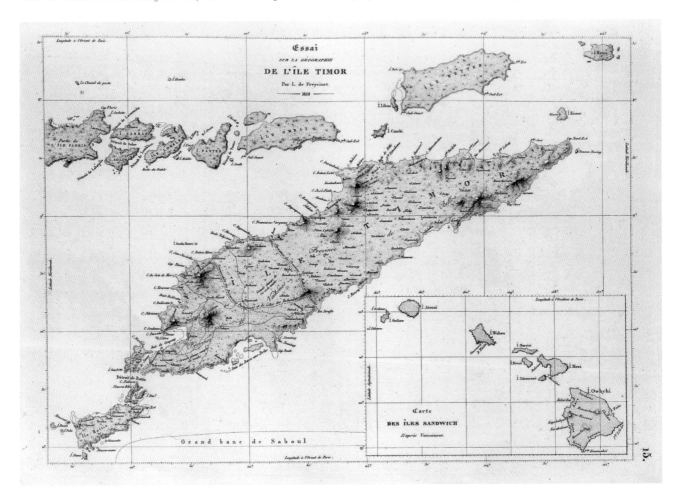

Descné par Marchais d'après A.Pellion.　　Gravé par Forget.

NOUVELLE-HOLLANDE, Baie des Chiens marins. CAMP DE L'URANIE, SUR LA PRESQU'ÎLE PÉRON.

**ABOVE:** Freycinet's camp at Shark Bay, Western Australia. After months aboard ship, the crewmen were pleased to spend as much time ashore as possible.

**RIGHT:** A peaceful scene along the shoreline of Matavai Bay on the north coast of Tahiti. By the time of Duperrey, Tahitian culture had changed forever with the arrival of whalers, merchants, and then missionaries.

**OPPOSITE:** Map of Timor and nearby islands that today are part of Indonesia, as drawn on Freycinet's voyage, with (inset) the Sandwich Islands, now the Hawaiian Islands.

**OVERLEAF:** Bora Bora in the Leeward group of the Society Islands, from Duperrey's voyage. Only 12 square miles (30 km²), it was first sighted by Europeans in 1722 on a Dutch expedition led by Jacob Roggeveen.

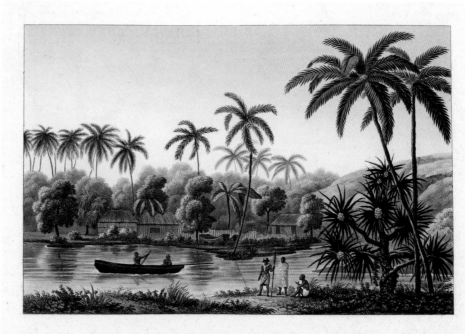

VUE D'UNE PARTIE DU VILLAGE DE MATAVAE, ILE DE TAÏTI.

Lejeune et Chazal delin.t

VUE DE I

(ILES

Ambroise Tardieu sculp.

BORABORA.

(OCIÉTÉ)

*Rhea Darwinii.*

# ROBERT FITZROY AND CHARLES DARWIN

## VOYAGE OF *BEAGLE*, 1831–36

IN THE EARLY NINETEENTH CENTURY, NAVIGATIONAL CHARTS WERE UNRELIABLE. CAPTAIN THOMAS HURD, THE HYDROGRAPHER OF THE NAVY, THEREFORE BEGAN TO RECRUIT OFFICERS CAPABLE OF CONDUCTING DETAILED SURVEYS OF SEAS AND COASTLINES. THESE SURVEYS WERE THEN TURNED INTO ACCURATE NAUTICAL CHARTS THAT COULD BE USED BY THE ROYAL NAVY IN BOTH PEACETIME AND WAR.

In 1826, Phillip Parker King was appointed to conduct a survey of the South American coast in HMS *Adventure*, which was accompanied by HMS *Beagle*, a specially built brig-sloop under the command of Pringle Stokes. Two years later, Stokes committed suicide and was replaced by Lieutenant Robert FitzRoy (1805–65). Eight months after returning to Britain, FitzRoy was placed in command of a new survey. He promptly set about having *Beagle* refitted, mostly at his own expense.

His expedition sailed from Plymouth in December 1831 with a complement of 75 men, including a young naturalist named Charles Darwin (1809–82), who had been recommended by John Stevens Henslow, professor of botany at Cambridge. The ship arrived at Rio de Janeiro in April 1832, having made stops at Madeira, Tenerife, the Cape Verde Islands and eastern Brazil. In the next three weeks, Darwin investigated the tropical rain forest – collecting insects and plants that were more diverse than he had ever imagined. Meanwhile, FitzRoy surveyed the coast north of Rio.

In July, *Beagle* continued to Buenos Aires, where FitzRoy began using smaller boats to survey rivers and dangerously shallow inlets. Several months later, they sailed south to Tierra del Fuego, where three Fuegians who had been brought to England by the previous cruise were returned home.

For the next year and a half, *Beagle* sailed up and down the east coast of South America, from Cape Horn to Montevideo and back to Tierra del Fuego, with several stops in the Falkland Islands and an extended cruise in three whale boats up the Rio Santa Cruz. In March 1833, while in the Falklands, FitzRoy bought a sealing schooner out of his own pocket, renamed her *Adventure*, and used her to extend his survey. All the while, Darwin visited as many environments as he could, collecting a vast array of specimens.

Finally, in June 1834, the two ships sailed through the Strait of Magellan and the Magdalen Channel into the Pacific Ocean. They

*Pyrocephalus nanus*

P. rubinus nanus Gould

**ABOVE:** Vermillion flycatcher from the Galapagos Islands by John Gould. Gould classified many of the the bird specimens brought back by Charles Darwin and illustrated them for *Zoology of the Voyage of H.M.S. Beagle*, edited by Darwin and published in five parts between 1838 and 1843.

**OPPOSITE:** Darwin's rhea (originally *Rhea darwinii*, now *Rhea pennata*), by Gould. A large, flightless bird from Patagonia and the Altiplano or Andean Plateau, it stands up to 39 inches (100 cm) tall and weighs up to 63 pounds (29 kg).

then headed north to Valparaiso. For the next two months, Darwin travelled through central Chile, but for the following three months he was bedridden. While he was incapacitated, FitzRoy received a message from the Admiralty, chastizing him for purchasing *Adventure* without official permission. Outraged, FitzRoy decided to sell the ship and resign his command. Fortunately, his officers were able to convince him to reconsider his future, and the expedition continued.

In November, Darwin rejoined *Beagle*, which cruised south to the island of Chiloe. In February 1835, she visited Valdivia. Not long after her arrival an earthquake devastated nearby Concepión and a resulting tsunami destroyed Talcahuano.

After sailing north to Callao, where they remained for six weeks, FitzRoy turned west to the Galapagos. Here they charted the main islands by means of small survey boats, while Darwin

**RIGHT:** Long-tailed sparrow (*Ammodramus longicaudatus*). Darwin saw these in Maldonado, Uruguay, noting that "this bird frequented, in small flocks, reeds and other aquatic plants bordering lakes ... It appears to live entirely on insects."

**BELOW:** A land iguana endemic to the Galapagos Islands, illustrated by Benjamin Waterhouse Hawkins for *Zoology of the Voyage of H.M.S Beagle*. It was originally designated *Amblyrynchus demarlii*, but is now *Conolophus subcristatus*.

*Ammodramus longicaudatus*

*Amblyrynchus Demarlii.* Nat. size.

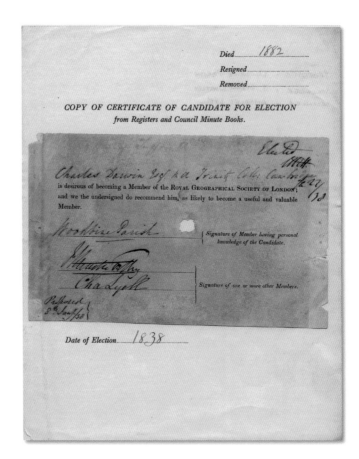

made collections that would be the basis for his future theories. Crossing the Pacific, *Beagle* stopped at Tahiti, New Zealand and several parts of Australia, before moving on to Mauritius, Cape Town, the Atlantic islands and, finally, England, which Darwin never left again.

For a period, FitzRoy's career went from strength to strength. He published his expedition account in 1839, and two years later was elected to Parliament. He served as governor-general of New Zealand, as superintendent at Woolwich dockyard, and then became the director of meteorology for the Board of Trade, where he made great advances in weather forecasting. He was eventually promoted to vice-admiral. When Darwin published *On the Origin of Species* in 1859, he was greatly troubled. Dogmatic in his religious views, he remained guilt-ridden by his contribution to the development of Darwin's theories for the rest of his life.

**ABOVE:** Darwin's pocket sextant carried throughout the voyage. Stored in a brass case, it was presented to the RGS by Darwin's son Leonard in 1912, shortly after he had served as the Society's president.

**TOP RIGHT:** Darwin's certificate of candidacy for election to the Royal Geographical Society. Proposed in January 1838 by Sir Woodbine Parish – an international diplomat, geologist, and palaeontologist – he was elected that month.

## DARWIN'S AND FITZROY'S ACCOUNTS FROM THEIR PERSONAL JOURNALS

When *Beagle* reached the Galapagos archipelago, both FitzRoy and Darwin wrote about the flora and fauna, each mentioning the role of the creator in making such unusual life forms – a distinctly different view than Darwin would espouse 25 years later. After staying on Charles Island (now Floreana Island) for a week, Darwin wrote:

*I industriously collected all the animals, plants, insects & reptiles from this Island. It will be very interesting to find from future comparison to what district or "centre of creation" the organised beings of this archipelago must be attached.*

Meanwhile, FitzRoy noted that:

*All the small birds that live on these lava-covered islands have short beaks, very thick at the base, like that of a bullfinch. This appears to be one of those admirable provisions of Infinite Wisdom by which each created thing is adapted to the place for which it was intended.*

R.Kirk
1841.

Falls of the Beraiza near Debra Berhan.

# RUPERT KIRK

## ARTIST IN THE ARABIAN PENINSULA AND ABYSSINIA, 1832–43

ALTHOUGH OFFICIALLY A MEMBER OF THE INDIAN MEDICAL SERVICE, RUPERT KIRK (1806–52) WAS ALSO ONE OF THE MOST TALENTED ARTISTS AMONG THOSE WHO WENT TO FARAWAY AND DANGEROUS PLACES ON BEHALF OF THE BRITISH EMPIRE. HE QUALIFIED AS A PHYSICIAN IN 1829, AND THE NEXT YEAR BECAME AN ASSISTANT SURGEON STATIONED IN BOMBAY (NOW MUMBAI).

In July 1832, Kirk was officially placed at the disposal of the Indian navy, which assigned him to the survey ship *Benares*, then in the region of the Arabian Peninsula and often based out of Mocha in Yemen. In the ensuing years he painted and drew many scenes, both coastal and at inland destinations near the survey sites, including Yemen, the region that is now Saudi Arabia, the Red Sea, Egypt and the Sudan. His watercolours not only communicate a remarkable sense of place, but the detail is rich in the kind of information that the agents of empire were eager to acquire.

In 1838, Kirk was appointed to the 1st Grenadier Regiment of the Bombay Native Infantry. He was thereafter assigned to the troops that formed part of the British force invading Afghanistan. Despite being plagued by a severe shortage of supplies, the army managed to capture Kandahar without firing a shot. Kirk then attended the action at the fortress of Ghazni, which saw the British troops win the day despite losing 200 men. Kirk returned to India when the majority of British troops withdrew from Afghanistan in late 1839.

**OPPOSITE:** The falls of the Beraiza river near the town of Debra-Berhan (now Debre Berhan). Located about 25 miles (40 km) from Ankober, the town later served as the Shoan (now Shewan) capital.

**BELOW:** The Bab-el-Mandeb, the strait located between what are today Yemen and Djibouti. It means "Gate of Tears", from, according to Arab legend, those drowned by the earthquake that separated Abyssinia from Arabia.

View of Mocha from the jetty from an original drawing by Lieut Carless I.N.    R Kirk. 1833. Aden &c

Kirk was next named a member of the mission led by Captain William Cornwallis Harris to the Shoa kingdom in the mountainous centre of Abyssinia (now Ethiopia). The mission was sent by the East India Company to work out a friendship and trade treaty with its king, Sahle Selassie. The party initially consisted of a 10-man negotiation and scientific team and their military escort.

Harris's party sailed from Bombay to Aden in April 1841, and landed the next month at the bay of Tajoora on the coast of what is today Djibouti. In the following weeks, they hired about 150 camels and their handlers, to haul their supplies and the gifts for Sahle Selassie. As they required far more camels to carry all of their stores, only Harris, Kirk, Captain Douglas Graham and two other members of the negotiating party continued with half the escort on the dangerous journey to the Shoan capital at Ankober. The other members of the team and the escort came with the remaining supplies after more camels had been obtained.

While en route to Ankober, Kirk kept a detailed diary, with notes about the geography, flora and fauna, and peoples and villages along the way, as well as meteorological and geological observations. Throughout the journey, he also painted and drew scenes of the more striking areas and features they passed.

After a week or so, three of the escort were killed in a night-time raid by the members of a local tribe. The party continued on

its rugged trek of 370 miles (595 km), including 10 days during which they had to manage without finding water. In mid-July the road became too difficult for camels, so their baggage was carried by 200 porters the final distance to a large village near Ankober. There the delegation had to remain in a "wretched, barn-like house" for more than two weeks until summoned to meet the king.

For the next year and a half, Harris and Graham negotiated with Sahle Selassie, while the other members of the embassy party compiled a wide range of scientific data. They were able to travel throughout the region, and Kirk produced numerous evocative images of the people and places. When the treaty was finally signed, the members of the mission returned to India, reaching it in May 1843. Kirk's contributions to the mission did not go unnoticed, and in 1845 he was promoted to full surgeon.

**ABOVE:** A view of Mocha in what today is Yemen. Mocha was the region's principal port until Aden surpassed it in the nineteenth century. Based on an original sketch by a Lieutenant Carless.

**OPPOSITE:** A Shoan (now Shewan) warrior in full battle regalia. His Ahodama, or head ornament, was a silver bar from which hung silver chains. It could only be worn by one who had slain an enemy in battle.

Shoan Warrior

R. Kirk. 1842.

Cave at Goongoonee

R. Kirk

## KIRK'S ACCOUNT FROM THE GEOGRAPHICAL JOURNALS

Kirk published accounts of his journey from Tajoora to Ankober in the *Journal of the Royal Geographical Society* and the *Transactions of the Bombay Geographical Society*. At one point the initial party had to wait for the pack camels to catch up. Being in a region that was notoriously dangerous due to hostile inhabitants, they took shelter in a cave. However, the temperature inside rose to 110°F (43°C), so that night they slept outside, guarded by the escort.

*At two A.M. we were awoke by a fearful cry from the escort, who rushed to our quarter, and we found that whilst the sentry's back was turned, they had been attacked as they slept. On proceeding to the spot, we found two of them in the agonies of death. One had been stuck in the neck just below the ear, the other been stabbed in the abdomen; and an unfortunate Portuguese cook, who slept last in the row, had also received a wound from which*

*the intestines were protruding ... The remainder of the night was passed in melancholy converse on the fate of our comrades. They were two of the best and finest looking men we had, and, from their former occupations, to us invaluable; one having been a farrier, the other a worker in leather. The poor cook, too, had, it was evident, received his death wound. Esak and his men voluntarily commenced preparing the graves, piling up stones against the side of the rock; and before daylight, with a short but impressive prayer, they were consigned to their untimely tombs.*

*From subsequent inquiries, there could remain no doubt that the cold-blooded deed had been perpetrated by the Bedouins, who, stealing down a hollow in the bank, had stabbed them as they slept. No attempt at plunder appeared as an excuse for the crime; but their only object seems to have been to acquire that estimation and distinction amongst their tribe, only to be acquired by these savages by deeds of blood.*

**OPPOSITE:** The cave at Goongoonta, where Kirk and his party sheltered until the temperature became unbearable and they moved outside.

**BELOW:** Goongoonta: where two guards and the cook were murdered in June 1841 after they had left the cave to sleep outside.

R. Kirk.

Scene of the murder at Goongoonta. June 9. 1841.

Pirogues du Havre Dorey.

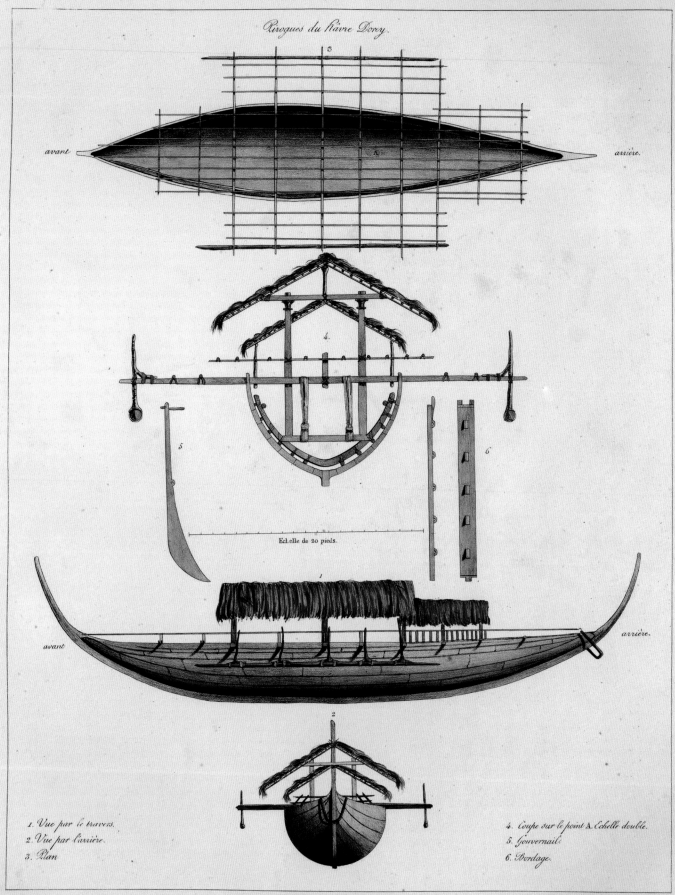

Echelle de 20 pieds.

1. Vue par le travers.
2. Vue par l'arrière.
3. Plan

4. Coupe sur le point A. Echelle double.
5. Gouvernail.
6. Bordage.

E. Paris pinx.

Siméon del.

J. Tastu Éditeur.

Lith. de Lemercier.

# JULES-SÉBASTIEN-CÉSAR DUMONT D'URVILLE

## VOYAGES OF *ASTROLABE* AND *ZÉLÉE*, 1826–29, 1837–40

AS A YOUNG NAVAL OFFICER, JULES-SÉBASTIEN-CÉSAR DUMONT D'URVILLE (1790–1842)
WAS ABLE TO PURSUE TWO OF HIS GREAT PASSIONS – BOTANY AND LINGUISTICS. (IN
ADDITION TO HIS NATIVE FRENCH, HE SPOKE ENGLISH, GERMAN, SPANISH, GREEK,
ITALIAN AND HEBREW.) HOWEVER, IT WAS FOR HIS INVOLVEMENT WITH FINE ART THAT HE
FIRST BECAME WIDELY KNOWN.

In 1819, as a junior officer aboard *Chevrette*, he visited the Greek island of Milos. There, via a chance conversation with a local peasant, he learned that an ancient statue had recently been unearthed. Visiting the site, he was overwhelmed by the statue's beauty and wrote to the French government pleading for them to purchase it. He received a positive response and, after fighting off several rival buyers, he arranged for it to be sent to the Louvre, where it was named the Venus de Milo.

Following that voyage, Dumont d'Urville was promoted to lieutenant, made a Chevalier de la Légion d'Honneur, and elected to the Linnean Society. He was then named second-in-command and botanist for Louis Duperrey's circumnavigation of the Earth on *Coquille* (1822–25). After that expedition returned to Marseilles, d'Urville proposed a new voyage, this time to study New Guinea and New Britain. The plan was approved – although his orders included also investigating Australia, New Zealand, Tonga and Fiji. Promoted to captain, he was given command of *Coquille*, which was then renamed *Astrolabe*.

The subsequent cruise lasted three years, during which parts of the Australian and New Zealand coasts, as well as numerous island groups, were charted. Clues from earlier voyagers prompted d'Urville to institute a search for the shipwreck from the grand expedition led by the Comte de La Pérouse, which had disappeared in 1788. First officer Charles-Hector Jacquinot eventually discovered the site at Vanikoro in the Solomon Islands.

*Astrolabe* returned to France with vast natural history collections, including 500 insects, 1,600 botanical specimens, 900 rock samples, and 3,350 drawings of 1,263 animals, many previously unknown to European science. Promoted to post captain, d'Urville spent the next six years producing an official expedition account, which comprised 12 written volumes and five albums of maps, charts and drawings.

**ABOVE**: Numerous forms of marine algae collected during Dumont d'Urville's first major expedition aboard *Astrolabe*.

**OPPOSITE**: A detailed diagram of a pirogue built near Dore Bay, New Guinea. Dumont d'Urville was fascinated by the locals' remarkable boat-handling abilities.

NOUVELLE-GUINÉE.

Pl. 125.

de Sainson pinx. et del.

Façade et détails de la maison sacrée à Dorey.

6 Pieds

J. Tastu, Éditeur.

Lith. de Lemercier.

VILLAGE DE KOKAOUI,
au Havre Dorey,
( N.lle Guinée.)

de Sainson pinx.

J. Tastu, Éditeur.

Sunqué del.

Lith. de Lemercier.

**ABOVE:** Details of a sacred house built in the waters of Dore Bay off New Guinea. *Astrolabe* reached there in August 1827 while carefully exploring the north shore of New Guinea and its surrounding islands.

**LEFT:** A seaside village in Dore Bay, New Guinea. The drawing was by Louis-Auguste de Sainson, who produced nearly 500 sketches during the 1826–29 voyage. Many of these appeared in the offical expedition account that he helped produce.

**OPPOSITE:** Dumont d'Urville's second expedition made an early sighting of Elephant Island, which was later made famous on Ernest Shackleton's Imperial Trans-Antarctic Expedition.

Early in 1837, he submitted a plan for yet another voyage of exploration to the Pacific. But King Louis-Philippe suggested that there was more opportunity for geographical discovery in the Antarctic. D'Urville was therefore ordered to take two ships as far south from the South Shetland Islands as possible and then to return via the Pacific.

Once again sailing in *Astrolabe*, and with Jacquinot in command of her consort *Zélée*, d'Urville made his way to the Antarctic. For two months they attempted to proceed beyond the South Orkneys or South Shetlands, but they were always thwarted by heavy ice. They discovered and named Joinville and D'Urville islands off the tip of the Antarctic Peninsula, but so many of the crew became debilitated by scurvy that the officers had to work the rigging. When a sailor died on 1 April 1838, d'Urville ordered a retreat to Chile so that his men could regain their health.

The ships next made their way across the Pacific, spending a year and a half exploring many island groups. On 2 January 1840, they sailed south from Hobart in Van Diemen's Land, and within about two weeks were surrounded by giant icebergs.

On 21 January they spied snow-covered land, and sailed west to where they could see bare rock in an offshore archipelago. The expedition's geologists were then sent ashore to collect samples. The coast was named Terre Adélie, after d'Urville's wife Adéle. On 29 January, the ships encountered *Porpoise*, part of the United States Exploring Expedition under Charles Wilkes.

After charting several hundred miles of Antarctic coastline, the French returned to Hobart in preparation for a nine-month voyage back to France. Upon reaching Toulon, d'Urville was promoted to admiral and awarded the gold medal of the Société de Géographie. Instructed by the King to write an expedition account, he had completed three volumes and the first three chapters of the fourth when, in May 1842, he, his wife, and their only son were killed in a railway accident.

London, Published by F.G.Moon, 20 Threadneedle Str. Nov. 1st 1846.

TOMBS OF THE KHALIFS, CAIRO.

# DAVID ROBERTS

## ARTIST OF EGYPT AND THE NEAR EAST, 1838–39

ALTHOUGH DAVID ROBERTS (1796–1864) SPENT LESS THAN A YEAR SKETCHING IN EGYPT AND THE NEAR EAST, HIS ARTWORK NOT ONLY STANDS AS SIGNIFICANT HISTORICAL DOCUMENTATION BUT HAS ENJOYED AN ENDURING POPULARITY WITH BOTH CRITICS AND THE PUBLIC FOR NIGH ON TWO CENTURIES.

He was born near Edinburgh to a family that struggled financially, and an early talent for drawing led to him being apprenticed to a house painter and decorator. Upon the completion of his apprenticeship, he became a scene painter for a touring company producing pantomimes. His success led to a series of jobs over the next 14 years, painting background scenes for a variety of major theatres, including in Edinburgh, Glasgow and London.

In 1824, Roberts travelled to France and his paintings of Rouen Cathedral subsequently won acclaim: purchased by the wealthy gin distiller Sir Felix Booth and the art collector Baron Northwick, they were also exhibited at the Royal Academy. He followed this with other trips to the Continent in the following decade. Many of his drawings from these journeys were reproduced as lithographic prints, which sold well and earned him great respect. Meanwhile, the famed artist J.M.W. Turner helped convince him to abandon scene painting and concentrate on fine art.

In 1838–39, Roberts fulfilled a childhood desire "to visit the remote East". After travelling to Alexandria and Cairo, he visited the Pyramids at Giza and produced a sketch of the Sphinx that became one of his most famous images. He then sailed up the Nile to Abu Simbel, where he recorded the massive temples still partly buried in the shifting sands. On his way back north, Roberts sketched and produced watercolours of ancient temples and landscapes at Philae, Karnak, Luxor and Dendera.

Roberts' tour then took him through Sinai to Petra, and north to Hebron and Jerusalem. He visited the Dead Sea, Bethlehem, Baalbek and many places associated with the Bible. In May 1839, he sailed for London, taking with him 272 individual sketches, a panorama of Cairo, and three additional full sketchbooks – enough material, he wrote, to "serve me for the rest of my life". Not long after his return he was elected a full member of the Royal Academy.

Excavated Temple of Gyrshe. Nubia

**OPPOSITE:** One of the tombs of the Caliphs in the "City of the Dead" on the outskirts of Cairo. Created in the seventh century, the Islamic necropolis was the preferred burial site for caliphs and later the Mamluk and Ottoman sultans.

**ABOVE:** The excavated temple of Gerf Hussein, called by Roberts the Temple of Gyrshe. Located in Nubia, some 55 miles (90 km) south of Aswan, it was built for Ramesses II in the thirteenth century BC.

For the next decade, Roberts produced paintings from his sketches, which were in turn made into coloured lithographs by the engraver Louis Haghe for six volumes of prints, published as *The Holy Land, Syria, Idumea, Arabia, Egypt and Nubia* between 1842 and 1846; and *Egypt and Nubia*, 1846–49.

Not only did these produce the most comprehensive visual account yet of the peoples, landscapes and ancient monuments of Egypt and the Near East, they were, according to the art critic and essayist John Ruskin, "the first studies ever made conscientiously by an English painter, not to exhibit his own skill, or make capital out of his subjects, but to give true portraiture of scenes of historical and religious interest." They also included, according to Ruskin, "attention and indefatigable correctness in detail". The lithographs became highly popular with the public as well as art collectors.

In the following years, Roberts again made his way to Western Europe, but his new paintings were never as successful as those from Egypt. In fact, Ruskin criticized them savagely – as described by the painter W.P. Frith in his autobiography:

*the critic wrote a private note to the artist ... [with] the expression of a hope that severe criticism would not interfere with the sincere feeling of friendship which the writer hoped would always exist ... To this Roberts replied that the first time he met the critic he would give him a sound thrashing; and he ventured to "hope that a broken head would not interfere with the sincere feeling of friendship which he hoped would always exist."*

Other critics through the years have been more positive about Roberts' artwork. *The Times* called him, "the best architectural painter that our country has yet produced", and a review in *The Guardian* commented that "His pictures ... take your breath away."

**OPPOSITE:** The gateway of the Great Temple at Baalbec. Known in antiquity as Heliopolis, the city is the home of some of the best-preserved Roman ruins in Lebanon, including the Temple of Bacchus.

**BELOW:** An encampment of the Aulad-Sa'id at Mount Sinai. The Aulad-Sa'id were a highly respected clan of Bedouin, who occupied a number of mountain valleys in Sinai.

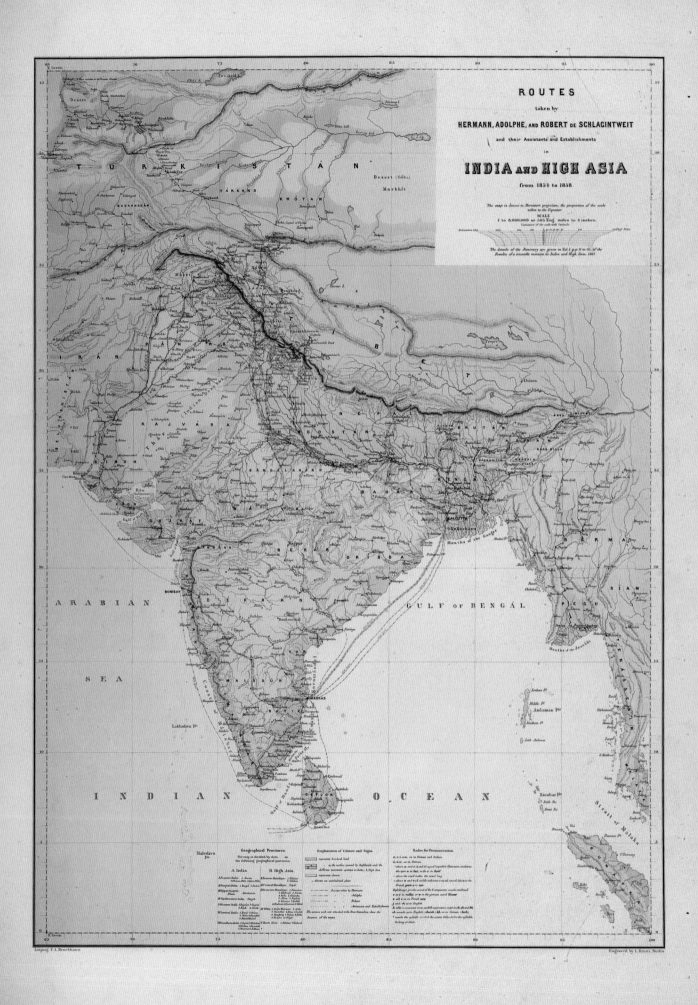

ROUTES
taken by
HERMANN, ADOLPHE, AND ROBERT DE SCHLAGINTWEIT
and their Assistants and Establishments
in
INDIA AND HIGH ASIA
from 1854 to 1858.

The map is drawn in Mercator's projection, the proportion of the scale
refers to the Equator

SCALE
1 to 8,000,000 or 505 Eng. miles to 4 inches.
Variation of the scale with latitude.

The details of the Itinerary are given in Vol.I. p.p. 11 to 35, of the
Results of a scientific mission to India and High Asia. 1861

# THE SCHLAGINTWEIT BROTHERS

## THE SCIENTIFIC EXPLORATION OF INDIA, 1854–57

FEW FAMILIES HAVE PRODUCED SO MANY CONTRIBUTORS TO THE HISTORY OF PHYSICAL GEOGRAPHY AS THE SCHLAGINTWEIT BROTHERS, THE SONS OF AN EMINENT EYE SPECIALIST IN MUNICH. FOUR OF THE FIVE BROTHERS MADE SIGNIFICANT CONTRIBUTIONS TO KNOWLEDGE ABOUT INDIA AND THE MOUNTAINS AND REGIONS NORTH OF IT.

At a young age, the eldest son, Hermann (1826–82), became fascinated by the natural history of the Alps, particularly the little-studied local glaciers. His brother Adolf (1829–57) soon joined him in his research and on trips to the mountains. Hermann's first paper about glaciers was published in 1847, and three years later he and Adolf produced a highly significant study of Alpine glaciers, geology, meteorology and botany. The next year, they made the second ascent of what was thought to be the eastern summit of the highest peak of the Monte Rosa Massif in the Swiss Alps.

Their scholarly work and outdoor experience brought them to the attention of Alexander von Humboldt, whom Hermann came to know better when he began lecturing at Berlin University. The brothers produced another important paper in 1854, to which the family's fourth son, Robert (1833–85), also contributed. That same year, with the recommendation of Humboldt and the backing of Kaiser Friedrich Wilhelm IV, the three were commissioned by the East India Company to conduct geomagnetic measurements, make ethnographical studies, and compile natural history collections throughout the Indian subcontinent. They also hoped to determine if the Himalayas were glaciated; current thinking suggested they were not.

The three sailed together to Bombay (now Mumbai), arriving in October 1854. Travelling separately for most of the next year, each took measurements in different parts of the Deccan, the plateau that makes up much of southern India. After finishing this part of their research, they met in Madras (now Chennai), from where they moved north to Calcutta (now Kolkata).

The brothers then split up again. Hermann made his way north through Bengal, eventually arriving at the mountain city of Darjeeling. From there he journeyed to the Brahmaputra River, which he followed into Assam. He then turned north into Bhutan before returning in March 1856 to Calcutta.

Meanwhile, Adolf and Robert headed northwest, following the Ganges and making for Nainital, a hill station where they spent six weeks conducting magnetic research. After exploring the western Himalayas and parts of the Karakoram, they continued beyond the East India Company's territories onto the high Tibetan Plateau, where they reached the lakes Manasarovar and Rakas Tal. Fleeing from Tibetans guarding their mysterious realm, they took separate routes to Simla, where they remained through the spring of 1856.

In May that year, Adolf and Robert were joined in Simla by Hermann. Posing as cotton and wool merchants, the three set off for Leh in Ladkah. Adolf went via the high passes and Hermann's route took him past a series of salt lakes. Meeting in Leh, they headed north and crossed the barren Depsang Plains at an elevation of about 17,400 feet (5,300 m). With seven of their 19 horses joining the trail of bones of countless pack animals that had died along the way, they crossed over the Karakoram Pass onto the Tibetan Plateau. They then became the first Europeans to cross the Kunlun Shan, the long mountain chain that divides the plateau from the Tarim Basin.

Turning about, they made their ways separately to Srinagar and continued together to Rawalpindi in what is today Pakistan. The brothers then separated for the final time, with Hermann travelling to Nepal before returning south to Calcutta. In April 1857, he sailed for Egypt, where he met Robert, who had taken most of their collection on a more direct route – south to Karachi and thence to Bombay before boarding a ship to Alexandria.

**OPPOSITE:** A map showing the numerous journeys of the Schlagintweit brothers in the Indian subcontinent and the mountains of central Asia.

Meanwhile, fascinated by what he had seen on the outskirts of the Tarim Basin, and hoping to return to Germany via central Asia and Russia, Adolf followed their previous route over the Karakoram and Kunlun Shan. Descending the mountains, he headed for the ancient Silk Road city of Kashgar. Shortly before reaching it, he was taken prisoner by the forces of the brutal Wali Khan, briefly the ruler there during a time of civil war. Suspected of being a spy for the Chinese, Adolf was beheaded in August 1857. It was only two years later that the circumstances of his death became known in Europe, after the Kazakh scholar Chokan Valikhanov visited Kashgar disguised as a merchant and returned with the scientist's head. Three decades later, the head's return inspired a scene in Rudyard Kipling's novella *The Man Who Would Be King*.

In June 1857, Hermann and Robert reached Trieste with 38 volumes of meteorological observations, 46 volumes of notes, 752 drawings and watercolours, and more than 14,000 natural history specimens. In the next six years they produced a four-volume scientific account of their expedition, which was published in German several years after it appeared in English.

Following the publication of their scientific results, Robert was named professor of geography at the University of Giessen. He made several trips to the United States and wrote a number of geographical accounts, in addition to a study about the Mormons in Utah. Hermann spent most of his time writing and administering the brothers' enormous collection from the family estate near Forchheim in northern Bavaria.

The youngest Schlagintweit brother, Emil (1835–1904), followed in his siblings' footsteps, travelling in northern India and becoming a respected orientalist. His book *Buddhism in Tibet* was long considered a classic. After his brothers died, he inherited the family estate, including his brothers' works and collections of Tibetan manuscripts. He later sold these to the Bodleian Library.

The middle brother, Eduard (1831–66), was a Bavarian army officer, who recorded geographical and ethnographic data while an official observer during the Spanish-Moroccan War. He was killed fighting against Prussia at the Battle of Kissingen.

The Buddhist monastery Himis, near Leh, in Ladák.

**Gaurisánkar, or Mount Everest, in the Himálaya of Nepál.**

Lat. North: 27°59'17"   Long. East of Green: 86°56'49"   Height: 29,000 Engl. feet

This is the highest mountain of our globe as yet measured. The drawing is taken from a mountain south-east of Falut, at a height of 11,025 Engl. feet. As a mighty massif it forms the prominent group of this view, though surrounded by some peaks of a height exceeding 20,000 Engl. feet. From its proximity to the tropics it stands out, as represented here at midday, in summer, a most conspicuous object in the full rays of a nearly vertical sun, herein exhibiting a highly characteristic feature, and presenting at the same time a most marked difference from the appearance of the Alpine peaks in higher latitudes. A very extensive glacier, of which the upper cirque de névé is seen on the left, descends to the south-west. The name given to Gaurisánkar by the Tibetans, and by which it is generally known to the natives in the northernmost parts of Nepál, is Chingopámari.

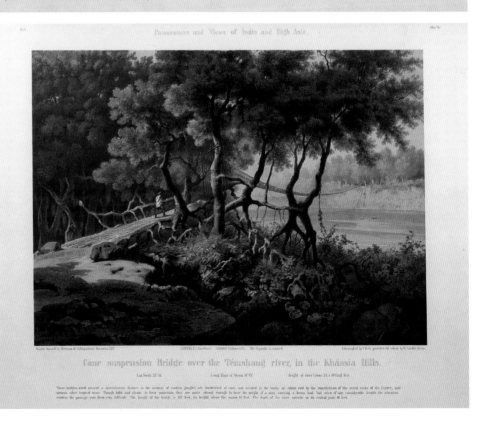

**Cane suspension Bridge over the Témshang river, in the Khássia Hills.**

Lat. North: 25°34'   Long. East of Green: 91°52'   Height of river (Géma): 311 x 50 Engl. feet

These bridges which present a characteristic feature in the scenery of eastern jungles are constructed of cane, and secured to the banks at either end by the ramification of the aereal roots of the Ficuses, and various other tropical trees. Though light and elastic in their materials, they are quite strong enough to bear the weight of a man carrying a heavy load, but when of any considerable length the vibrations renders the passage over them very difficult. The length of the bridge is 312 feet, its height above the water 62 feet. The depth of the river outside in its central parts 36 feet.

**OPPOSITE:** Buddhist monastery in Hemis, 28 miles (45 km) from Leh in Ladakh. The annual Hemis festival is still held there each June.

**RIGHT:** Cane suspension bridge over the Témshang River in the Khássia (today Khasi) Hills in what used to be Assam. The bridge was 312 feet (95 m) long and 62 feet (19 m) above the river.

**ABOVE:** Mount Everest, which Hermann Schlagintweit wrote was also called Gaurisankar. In 1903, a survey proved that Everest and Gaurisankar are different peaks, 36 miles (58 km) apart.

Original Aquarell by Hermann de Schlagintweit, July, 1856.

Leh, the

Lat. North: 34°8′5

This town, situated three miles north of the Indus, is the largest in West
The imposing edifice, seven stories high, which rises above the surrounding
histic religious buildings, such as chórtens and prayer-walls, are scattered all
and remained in the occupation of our establishment during our absence in Ti

**RIGHT**: A view of Leh, the capital of Ladakh,
when visited by the Schlagintweit brothers.
Located in what was then western Tibet, it
was a key centre for trade between central
Asia and India.

Lithographed by C.Koch, printed in Oil-colours by W. Loeillot, Berlin.

## al of Ladák, in Western Tibet.

Long. East of Green: 77° 14′ 36″            Height: 11,527 Engl. feet

a most important place for the trade between Central Asia and India. The houses have flat roofs, on which small tents are sometimes pitched. ient residence of the former rulers of Ladák, and by its prominent position commands the whole of the town. Several monasteries, and numerous Budd- and its environs. The large house on the left, at the entrance to the town, with the two tents on its roof, was the residency inhabited by us, er when caravans, from distant regions, meet at Leh, the number and variety of tribes and creeds is remarkably great for a town so far remote in the in

terior of a vast continent.

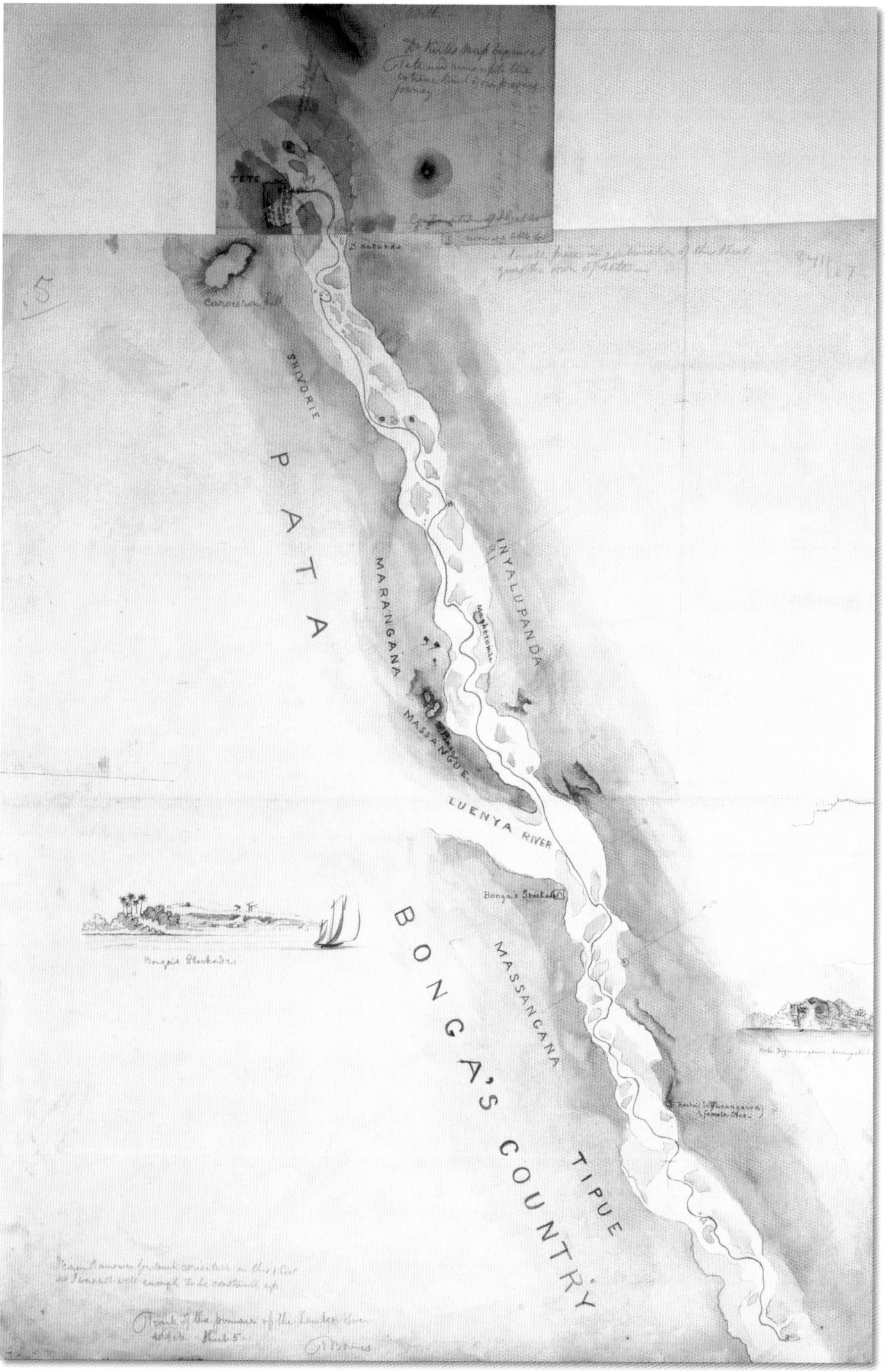

North

Dr Kirk's Map begins at
Tete and runs into this
by some kind of non sequity
journey

TETE

E. Matunda

Cararéron hill

Inselt press in subordinate of this sheet
gives the work of Tete

241/67

5

SHIVORIE

P A T A

MARANGANA

INYALU PANDA

MASSANGUE

LUENYA RIVER

Bonga's Stockade

B O N G A' S   C O U N T R Y

T I P U E

M A S S A N G A N A

Bonga's Stockade

Rocks (N'Vacangaira)
(female Ibex)

I regret answer for such correction in this Ch'l
as I inward will enough to be carried up

Rough of the summer of the Zambesi River
White Kurt 5

# DAVID LIVINGSTONE
## ZAMBEZI EXPEDITION, 1858–64

DAVID LIVINGSTONE (1813–73) WAS ONE OF THE MOST REVERED OF BRITISH IMPERIAL HEROES. BORN INTO WHAT WAS CALLED "THE RESPECTABLE POOR", HE BEGAN WORKING IN A COTTON MILL AT THE AGE OF 10. DESPITE WORKING 13 HOURS A DAY, SIX DAYS A WEEK, HE GAINED A SOLID EDUCATION BY STUDYING AT NIGHT.

Deciding to be a medical missionary, he qualified while supporting himself by continuing to work at the mill. In 1840, at the age of 27, he finished his medical training and was ordained a minister, and then sailed for South Africa.

Livingstone found converting Africans to Christianity extremely difficult, and realized that he was drawn to explore the continent's unknown interior. In 1849, he was the first European to reach Lake Ngami, and six years later the first to see the magnificent cascade that he named Victoria Falls. At the same time, he developed a complex plan to spread Christianity, fight the slave trade and open new territories for British trade. By the mid-1850s, he had become a strange melange: part social theorist, part explorer, part propagandist, part trading expansionist, and part anti-slavery proponent. What he needed next was to become a figure whose voice would be heard.

This was accomplished between 1853 and 1856, when he made the first crossing of Africa by a European. When he returned to Britain, he was hailed as a hero. Roderick Murchison, the president of the Royal Geographical Society (RGS), called his explorations "the greatest triumph in geographical research effected in our times". Livingstone received the Founder's Medal of the RGS, was elected to the Royal Society, and had an audience with the Queen.

One of the key reasons for Livingstone's emergence as a national hero was his backing by Murchison, who believed he could

**RIGHT**: Thomas Annan's famous photograph of Livingstone and his youngest daughter, Anna Mary. The picture reinforced Livingstone's image as a devoted family man, although he actually abandoned his family for many years at a time.

**OPPOSITE**: Thomas Baines' hand-drawn map of the route Livingstone took on the Zambezi in *Ma Robert*. This was part of the material that Livingstone refused to give credit for or to return to Baines after they parted company.

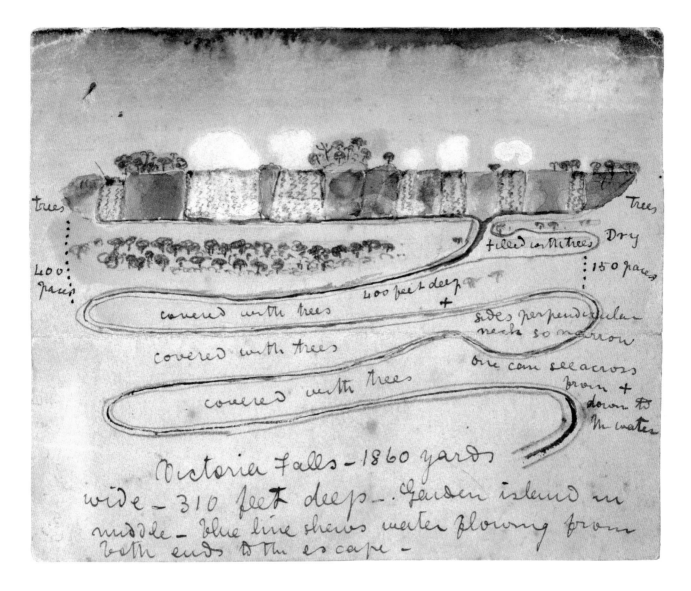

trees

400 paces

covered with trees

covered with trees

covered with trees

400 feet deep

filled in with trees

Dry

150 paces

sides perpendicular neck so narrow one can see across from + down to the water

Trees

Victoria Falls — 1860 yards wide — 310 feet deep — Garden island in middle — blue line shews water flowing from both ends to the escape —

be an asset to the RGS, particularly in attracting new members. Murchison was the major political force behind Livingstone's next expedition, the stated goals of which were to navigate the Zambezi River from the east coast to Victoria Falls in order to assess the Batoka Plateau's agricultural potential, promote trade, and establish missions.

Livingstone was given a free hand in choosing his staff, and among those he selected were geologist Richard Thornton, engineer George Rae, medical officer and botanist John Kirk, and Livingstone's brother Charles, serving as "moral agent" and photographer. Charles was thus the first official photographer on a British government-sponsored expedition. The expedition also included an extremely talented artist – Thomas Baines, who had worked for the RGS and had just received special acknowledgement from the colonial government for his role on Augustus Gregory's North Australian Expedition.

Livingstone's expedition sailed from Liverpool in March 1858, arriving at the mouth of the Zambezi two months later. Before long, Livingstone was met by a large contingent of Makololo

people, residents of a region high up the Zambezi, who had accompanied him to the village of Tete two years earlier. He had told them he would return in a year to guide them back home, and they had patiently waited for his return, even though it was a year longer than promised.

A purpose-built paddle-steamer of shallow draught was assembled and named *Ma-Robert* – after the name used by the Makololo for Livingstone's wife Mary. Tensions were high among the Britons from the start – primarily because Livingstone, who had not previously worked much with Europeans, proved not to understand them. He was brusque, moody, aloof, and openly

---

**ABOVE:** Livingstone's sketch of Victoria Falls. Livingstone wrote in his book: "It had never before been seen by European eyes; but scenes so lovely must have been gazed upon by angels in their flight."

**OPPOSITE TOP:** *Ma-Robert* aground at the head of the eastern branch of the West Luabo River. The steam-launch was nicknamed "The Asthmatic" because of the extensive problems with her boilers.

The Ma Robert aground at the head of the eastern branch of the West Luabo River. Monday May 24. 1858. *T. Baines*

**BELOW**: A sextant used by Livingstone in central Africa in the 1860s.

critical. It was not a combination of qualities destined to pull a party together, and after only two months, Norman Bedingfield, the expedition's second-in-command, was dismissed. In the end, it proved impossible for the boat to pass the Kebrabasa Rapids, which Livingstone had not seen on his trans-continental journey. This temporarily put an end to his dream of "an English colony in the healthy highlands of Central Africa".

In order to save face, Livingstone decided instead to investigate the Shire River, which flowed into the Zambezi about 90 miles (150 km) from the coast. On the first day of 1859, *Ma-Robert* entered the Shire, but eight days later was stopped by what Livingstone named the Murchison Cataracts. In the following months, Livingstone and Kirk explored the region on foot, and Livingstone became convinced that it would be suitable both for growing cotton and as the centre of new missionary work. In September they reached what they called Lake Nyasa (today Lake Malawi). This had already been seen by Portuguese explorers, but Livingstone claimed that *he* had discovered it.

For several months, Livingstone stayed put, waiting to hear if the government would extend what had been planned as a two-year mission – and if it would replace the leaky, underpowered *Ma-Robert*.

Meanwhile, Charles had proven extremely disagreeable, and was the reason that Thornton was sent home in June 1859. Later Charles accused Baines of stealing sugar, and although others in the party disputed it, Livingstone dismissed him as well. Worse yet from Baines' perspective, he was not allowed to return to the camp where his drawings were, and Livingstone retained them and later used them for his expedition account.

For much of 1860 Livingstone was busy repatriating the Makololo people, whom he had earlier brought down the Zambezi. During his return, he overrode objections by Charles and Kirk, and insisted on descending the Kebrabasa Rapids by canoe. Kirk almost drowned and lost his scientific instruments, notes and drawings. However, they reached their camp at Tete to find the

extension of the mission had been approved. The engineer Rae had already returned to Britain to supervise the building of a portable steamer that could be carried past the cataracts on the Shire River and then reassembled to travel on its upper stretches and Lake Nyasa.

Unfortunately, while Livingstone had been in the interior, disaster had struck other parts of the expedition. At his bidding, the London Missionary Society had sent two families to establish a mission at Linyanti on the Zambezi, but six of the nine had died before they arrived. Undaunted, Livingstone convinced the Church Missionary Society to send out a party under Bishop Charles Mackenzie. Its goal was to create mission stations on both the Zambezi and the Shire.

Mackenzie arrived at the coast in January 1861, along with *Pioneer*, the replacement for *Ma-Robert*, which Livingstone had abandoned on a sandbank. That summer, while Livingstone explored Lake Nysasa from a four-oared gig, the mission was

established in the nearby highlands. But its chosen site was highly malarial, and Mackenzie and several others died before the end of 1862. Their supplies were then destroyed by hostile slavers, and even more perished. Finally, in 1864, the mission was moved to Zanzibar.

In January 1862, the portable steamer, *Lady Nyassa*, arrived at the Zambezi, along with Livingstone's wife Mary and more missionaries. They moved upriver to Shupanga to assemble the ship, but in April, Mary contracted malaria. She died a week later. Livingstone now turned his attention to the Rovuma River, which he attempted to ascend first in *Pioneer* and then in open boats. He was unsuccessful in both.

At the beginning of January 1863, Livingstone's party sailed for the Shire River aboard *Lady Nyassa*. But the river was unusually

low and it was not until April that the ship managed to reach the Murchison Cataracts. By that time, most of the party had malaria, and a number had died. That month, both Charles and Kirk returned to England. Although a number of Kirk's photographs have survived, those taken by Charles were almost entirely lost.

In the following period, little advance was made upriver, and in July Livingstone received a despatch recalling the expedition. He ignored the order and, with Edward Young, captain of *Pioneer*, continued on foot to Lake Nyasa, where they explored its western shore.

They then returned to the mouth of the Zambezi, where Livingstone decided to sail *Lady Nyassa* to Zanzibar and sell her. He and Rae travelled the 1,500 miles (2,400 km) along the African coast in a ship designed only for river travel and worked by an inexperienced African crew. Somehow they reached Zanzibar in April 1864. Finding no buyer there, they made a remarkable 45-day journey under sail, travelling 2,500 miles (4,000 km) across the ocean to Bombay. From there, Livingstone boarded a ship for England.

Though the expedition could not be described as a total success, his spirit and drive were undaunted, and he would return to Africa again, searching for the sources of the Nile.

**ABOVE:** Local women producing containers to hold sugar at a village near Tete. Baines' careful depictions of the dress, activities, and living quarters of the people of the region are invaluable historic resources.

**OPPOSITE:** A point where the rapids at Kebrabasa divided into three fast-flowing channels. The river was not navigable through this region, bringing to an immediate halt the original plans of the expedition.

WHITE RHINOCEROS. *R. simus*
*R. simus* *S. Africa*

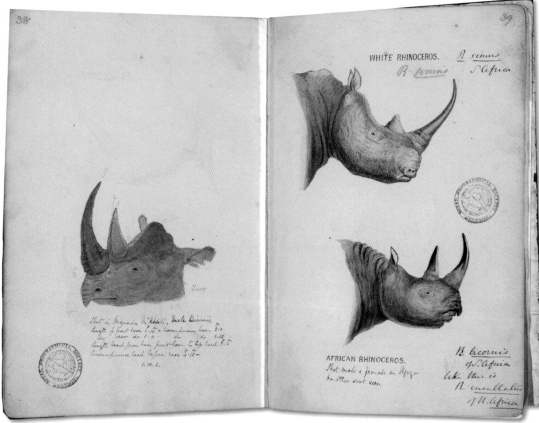

AFRICAN RHINOCEROS.
*Shot male & female in Mgogo*
*no other sort seen*

*B. bicornis*
*of S. Africa*
*like this is*
*B. cucullatus*
*of N. Africa*

# JOHN HANNING SPEKE AND JAMES AUGUSTUS GRANT

## SEARCH FOR THE SOURCE OF THE NILE, 1860–63

IT WAS STRICTLY FORTUITOUS THAT JOHN HANNING SPEKE (1827–64) BECAME AN AFRICAN EXPLORER. AN OFFICER IN THE EAST INDIAN COMPANY ARMY, HE HAD SERVED IN SEVERAL WARS AND HAD SPENT MUCH TIME HUNTING BIG GAME, WHEN HE HAPPENED TO MEET RICHARD FRANCIS BURTON IN ADEN. BURTON HAD A VACANCY ON HIS EXPEDITION TO SOMALIA AND THE CITY OF HARAR, AND SPEKE GLADLY ACCEPTED THE CHANCE TO JOIN HIM.

After serving in the Crimean War, Speke again joined Burton, this time to find the Sea of Ujiji (which Burton named Lake Tanganyika). The men left Zanzibar in June 1857, and eight months later reached the massive lake. They surveyed it, then made their way back to Tabora, the principal trading centre of inland East Africa. While Burton recovered from malaria and gathered information from Arab traders, Speke journeyed north to investigate rumours of another great lake. On 3 August 1858, he saw it and named it Victoria Nyanza (now Lake Victoria). He was immediately convinced that this was the source of the Nile. Unable to persuade Burton of this, Speke returned to London and consulted Roderick Murchison, the president of the Royal Geographical Society (RGS). Murchison immediately helped Speke to publicize his claims, making him a national hero and completing an already-growing breach with Burton.

Returning to England 13 days after Speke, Burton immediately disputed his colleague's claims. To settle the matter, the RGS sent Speke back to East Africa so that he could follow the Nile from the lake to Egypt, thus confirming that it truly was the river's source. As a companion, Speke selected James Augustus Grant (1827–92), another East India Company officer, whom he had met in 1847. Grant was a talented artist and a keen botanical collector.

Speke and Grant set out in October 1860 with a caravan of 213 men. Despite constant rain and a sickness that killed many mules, they reached Tabora in late January 1861. Throughout the expedition, both men suffered from numerous tropical ailments, which meant both that there were long periods where they were immobile and that they made parts of the journey separately. In addition, lengthy halts where required while negotiating with local leaders through whose territory the expedition had to pass.

In November they reached Karagwe, to the west of Victoria Nyanza. Two months passed before they were allowed to travel north into the kingdom of Buganda, ruled by the despot Mutesa. Speke proceeded to Mutesa's capital, near modern-day Kampala, north of the lake, which they had still not yet seen. Grant was suffering from an ulcerated leg and did not arrive until three months later. In July 1862, they were sent northwest, with an escort that took them directly to the Nile, but some 30 geographical miles (56 km) north of the lake.

As he had not yet proved the connection between Victoria Nyanza and the Nile, Speke followed the river back south. On

**OPPOSITE:** Pages from published books recording African animals, on which Speke and Grant made notes and, on the pages opposite, recorded their own sketches of the animals they had seen.

**BELOW:** Speke's drawing of the Ripon Falls, where the Nile emerged from Victoria Nyanza. The completion of the Owen Falls Dam in 1954 effectively extended Lake Victoria and submerged the falls.

28 July 1862, he reached the waterfalls where the Nile issues from the lake, naming them Ripon Falls after Sir Roderick Murchison's successor as RGS president. Unfortunately, Grant had continued north due to his bad leg, so there was no one to confirm the discovery, just as there had not been when Speke had originally reached Victoria Nyanza.

Once reunited, the two men continued north, but twice took shortcuts, not precisely following the river's course and thereby missing two significant sections of it. This allowed critics to question whether the river flowing from Victoria Nyanza was indeed the Nile, or if they had just joined it at a later stage.

In February 1863 the explorers arrived at Gondokoro, a station for the trade in ivory and slaves. There, Samuel and Florence Baker (see pages 68–71) willingly shared their supplies with them. Speke and Grant then continued downriver to Cairo, and returned to England in the summer of 1863.

Speke was lionized by the public upon his return, although Burton and other geographers claimed that the expedition had once again not conclusively proved the connection between Victoria Nyanza and the Nile. Indeed, the theory was not confirmed for another dozen years. By then, the Bakers had discovered the Albert Nyanza (1864), Charles Chaillé-Long had traced the Nile through the Lake Kyogo region that Speke had only skirted (1874), and Henry Morton Stanley had proved that Victoria Nyanza was one lake and not a collection of smaller ones (1875).

Speke had been right, but he never lived to see this proved. He died in a hunting accident in 1864.

**TOP:** The Wasagara Hills, an area in what is today Tanzania. After Speke wounded but could not catch an eland buck, he and Grant continued on through the Robého (or windy) Pass.

**ABOVE:** Illustration from the front cover of *The Illustrated London News* of 4 July 1863, showing the reception of Speke and Grant at the RGS, where they were honoured for their African journey.

**OPPOSITE:** Map of the route taken by Speke and Grant from Zanzibar to the Nile. It was drawn and coloured by Grant and includes an explanatory note added by Speke in February 1863.

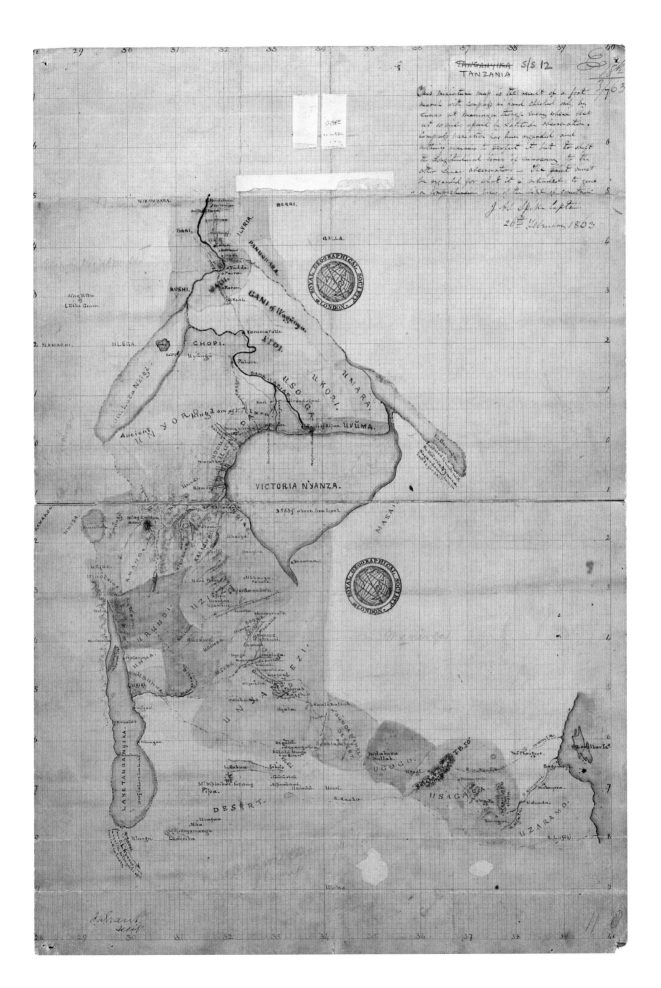

# THOMAS BAINES

## ARTIST AND EXPLORER OF SOUTHERN AFRICA, 1858-64

JOHN THOMAS BAINES (1820–75) CAME FROM AN ARTISTIC KING'S LYNN FAMILY – HIS
BROTHER HENRY WAS A PROFESSIONAL ARTIST KNOWN FOR PAINTINGS CELEBRATING THE
COUNTRYSIDE OF NORFOLK, AND HIS FATHER AND GRANDFATHER WERE TALENTED AMATEURS.
AT A YOUNG AGE, THOMAS (AS HE WAS KNOWN) WAS APPRENTICED TO A HERALDIC PAINTER,
WHO SPECIALIZED IN THE CRESTS, ARMS AND ANIMALS ON CARRIAGE DOORS.

In 1842, he moved to Cape Town, where he initially worked as an ornamental sign-painter. Three years later, he turned full-time to painting portraits and the wonders of nature.

In 1848, Baines began a series of journeys to the interior of Southern Africa, sketching and painting wildlife, scenery and the local population, while travelling first beyond the Orange River, then the Great Kei River and finally towards the marshes of the Okavango Delta. In 1850–51, he served as the British Army's official war artist during the Eighth Frontier War. A year later, he published a folio of lithographs of his paintings from the war, and also moved back to England, where he worked for the Royal Geographical Society (RGS).

In 1855, at the recommendation of the RGS, Baines was named the storekeeper and artist on Augustus Gregory's North Australian Expedition. Starting from the estuary of the Victoria River in the far north, the expedition explored parts of the Northern Territory, then continued east through Queensland to Gladstone, north of Brisbane. The journey on land covered more than 5,000 miles (8,000 km). At one point during the trek, Baines led an excursion of 700 miles (1,150 km) in an open boat to obtain provisions at Timor. His efforts were rewarded by a special vote of thanks from the colonial government, and the Baines River was named after him. His sketches and paintings showed him to be a gifted artist able to translate the beauties and mysteries of remote regions.

Shortly after he returned to England, the RGS recommended him for a place on David Livingstone's Zambezi Expedition (see pages 46–51) , again as artist and storekeeper. He made several ventures away from the main party, and sketched the scenery and local peoples as well as producing detailed maps. However, Baines did not get along with Livingstone's brother Charles, who unjustly accused him of stealing sugar. Livingstone dismissed Baines and did not allow him to retrieve his artwork, which was later used without acknowledgement by the Livingstone brothers in their account of the expedition.

After returning to Cape Town, Baines joined the trader and photographer James Chapman on an expedition from the west coast to Victoria Falls (1861–63). Chapman had been exploring the region for most of a decade and had travelled at times with Francis Galton and the Swedish explorer Charles Andersson in Namaqualand and Damaraland (in modern Namibia). In 1853 he had reached the Zambezi, but had turned back just short of discovering Victoria Falls, allowing Livingstone the honour of being the first European to reach it. Now, Chapman wanted to investigate

---

**OPPOSITE:** A set of sketches of the Griqua. A racially and culturally diverse people, they moved away from the growing Dutch and British influence and inhabited the interior regions of what are today South Africa and Namibia.

**BELOW:** Self-portrait of Baines perched in a baobab tree sketching the scenes in the vicinity of Lake Ngami. The piece was drawn in April 1862, during his and Chapman's slow progress to Victoria Falls.

**RIGHT**: Victoria Falls and the Zambezi River. Upon arriving, Baines wrote: "tell me if heart of man ever conceived anything more gorgeous than those two lovely rainbows, so brilliant that the eye shrinks from looking on them, segments of which rising from the abyss, deep as the solar rays can penetrate it, overarch spray, rock, and forest."

the possibility of navigating the upper Zambezi and establishing a chain of trading stations between there and Walvis Bay.

The journey to Victoria Falls took 16 months by ox-wagon, during which Baines made a thorough route survey, collected natural history specimens, and produced a large number of sketches and paintings, including his most famous – those of Victoria Falls. Technical problems prevented Chapman from taking photographs of the falls, which would be not photographed until 1891. It was this shortcoming that most distressed Chapman. Despite having experienced illness, drought and, at times, lack of food, he later wrote to Sir George Grey, the governor of the Cape Colony: "Of all our disappointments I regret none more deeply, and I am sure your Excellency will sympathise with me when I say that I come back without one good photograph."

Eventually, a series of heavy storms halted the expedition, as the wagons sank to their axles in mud. The rain also ruined some of the supplies, and with the expedition facing a spread of malaria, Chapman called a retreat. They returned to the coast the same way they had come, and Baines spent the next year with Andersson in Damaraland, sketching pictures of birds and other wildlife. Many of these were used by Andersson in his exhaustive study *Birds of Damara Land*.

Returning to England in 1864, Baines published his famous album of prints, *The Victoria Falls, Zambezi River Sketched on the Spot*. He again went to South Africa in 1867 and made two trips on behalf of the South African Goldfields Exploration Company to obtain a concession to hunt for gold from Lobengula, king of Matabeleland (in what is today Zimbabwe). In 1873, he investigated gold deposits in Natal and also attended the coronation of Cetshwayo as king of the Zulus. That same year, he was awarded a testimonial gold watch by the RGS. While writing an account of his South African expeditions, he fell ill, and died of dysentery. Later that year, Sir Henry Rawlinson, the president of the RGS, said of him that "few men were so well endowed … for successful African travel, and perhaps none possessed greater courage and perseverance or more untiring industry."

Baines produced many oil paintings, watercolours and sketches that today provide a window into colonial Africa and its inhabitants during the mid-nineteenth century. Because he annotated his works in remarkable detail – noting the time, date, place, and even the length of time that elapsed between the preliminary sketch and the final painting – they give a unique insight into how one artist worked at that time.

Quagga. young male (most probably new end to Equus Chapmanni)

**ABOVE:** A number of Bushmen (now known as San) hunting a herd of heterogeneous game. This image came from the time of Baines' assignment as a war artist with the British Army.

**RIGHT:** Baines identified this as a young male quagga, shot by Chapman. However, its markings suggest it was a Burchell's zebra rather than a quagga, which were striped at the front and solid brown throughout the rear, and are now extinct.

**OPPOSITE:** A baobab tree about 50 feet (15 m) tall on the trail to Lake Ngami. The species is extremely long-lived, with one living tree in South Africa carbon-dated to more than 1,700 years old.

# CARLETON WATKINS
## PHOTOGRAPHER OF THE AMERICAN WEST, 1861–90

RARELY HAS A SINGLE ARTIST OR PHOTOGRAPHER HAD A MAJOR INFLUENCE ON THE ESTABLISHMENT OF ANY LONG-TERM GOVERNMENT POLICY. HOWEVER, CARLETON WATKINS (1829–1916), A REMARKABLE RECORDER OF THE AMERICAN WEST, HAD JUST SUCH AN IMPACT – ONE STILL BEING POSITIVELY FELT 150 YEARS LATER.

Born in Oneonta, New York, Watkins was lured by the opportunities of the California Gold Rush, and around 1851 he moved to Sacramento. There he worked as a teamster and carpenter for the company of Collis Huntington, a friend from Oneonta who later became one of the "Big Four" owners of the Central Pacific Railroad. Two years later, Watkins moved to San Francisco, where he worked for Robert Vance, a well-known daguerreotypist with several studios. When the man running his San Jose studio unexpectedly left his job, Vance asked Watkins to look after it temporarily and showed him the basics of photography. By the time Vance next returned, Watkins had taught himself enough to become a successful portrait photographer.

After several years working for Vance, Watkins established his own business, and began producing photographs for engravings in *Illustrated California Magazine*. He also took photographs for the courts as evidence in land or mining disputes. His images documented the rapid growth of San Francisco, where he lived from 1853 to 1906.

From early in his career, Watkins experimented with new developments that would set him apart from the norm. One of these was a stereo camera that produced two identical images, and when viewed through a stereoscope, these produced a three-dimensional picture. This camera used a glass plate that was 5.5 x 14 inches (14 x 35.6 cm), and produced two negatives of 5.5 x 7 inches (14 x 17.8 cm) each.

Experimenting further, Watkins employed a cabinet-maker in 1861 to build a camera that measured 3 feet (91.4 cm) when extended and used what he called mammoth plates, which were 18 x 22 inches (45.7 x 55.9 cm). The giant negatives this camera produced allowed him to take pictures of subjects too large for normal cameras, thereby allowing him to capture the enormous scale of the American West.

**ABOVE**: Dwarfed by a magnificent redwood is Galen Clark, the first European-American to discover the Mariposa Grove of Giant Sequoias. He later played a major role in gaining legislation to protect it and Yosemite.

**OPPOSITE**: The southeast face of El Capitan, the pale granite monolith rising about 3,000 feet (900 m) from the valley floor. Named in 1851, today it is one of the world's greatest rock-climbing challenges.

That summer, Watkins transported his two unusual cameras – and a total of more than 2,000 pounds (900 kg) of equipment, all on a dozen mules – to the Sierra Nevada range. He visited Yosemite Valley, one of the most stunningly beautiful areas in North America, and the Mariposa Grove, a large group of giant sequoias, the world's most massive trees. In the following weeks he exposed 30 mammoth plates and about 100 stereoscopic negatives.

By 1863 Watkins' Yosemite images had gained a national reputation. Not only did they introduce the valley to the public of the eastern United States, but they were also considered of superb technical and artistic quality. At the same time, the success of these photographs won him a market for his images of San Francisco, the Mendocino County coast and the New Almaden mining region.

In 1864, California Senator John Conness used Watkins' Yosemite masterpieces when he sponsored an act to transfer Yosemite Valley and the Mariposa Grove to the state so that they might "be used and preserved for the benefit of mankind". The prints were instrumental in persuading Congress to pass legislation protecting Yosemite, and President Abraham Lincoln to sign the act that granted the valley and grove to California. Not only

is Lincoln's agreement considered *the* initial step in the creation of the U.S. National Park system, but it also effectively started the American conservation movement. Thus, although Mount Watkins in Yosemite was named in honour of his contributions, his environmental legacy is greater than the establishment of just one park.

Watkins returned to Yosemite in 1864 and 1865 on behalf of the California State Geological Survey. His use of a new wide-angle lens allowed him to expand his repertoire. He visited Yosemite again later in the decade and in the early 1870s. In 1867, he opened his first public gallery and also was awarded a medal for landscape photography at the Paris International Exhibition. That summer, he travelled up the Willamette and Columbia rivers, and his 136 stereographs and 60 mammoth plates from that journey are considered second only to his Yosemite images.

**OPPOSITE**: Yosemite Falls drops a total of 2,425 feet (739 m) from the top of the upper fall, through five smaller cascades, and down the lower fall.

**BELOW**: The splendour and majesty of Yosemite Valley, with bookends El Capitan and Half Dome, is shown in this image taken from Inspiration Point.

**LEFT**: The waters of the Merced River tumble down Nevada Fall, with a mid-fall collision with the rock face creating a broad misty appearance.

**OPPOSITE**: Half Dome, with the crest of its sheer northwest face some 4,737 feet (1,444 m) above the east Yosemite Valley, taken from Glacier Point.

**BELOW**: A map of Yosemite Valley, produced in 1865, after President Abraham Lincoln signed legislation giving it to the state of California.

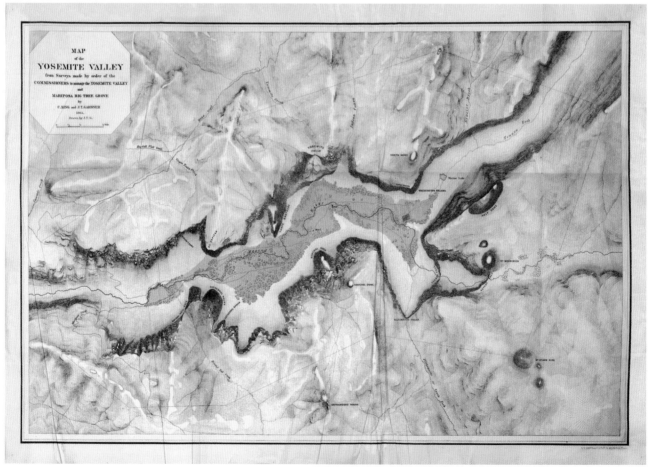

In the following years Watkins produced numerous views of the Pacific coast, Mount Shasta and the geysers of Sonoma County. He was supported in these travels by his old friend Collis Huntington, who allowed him to use a train flatcar to carry his photographic materials. Watkins' success allowed him to open a San Francisco studio named the Yosemite Art Gallery. But during the financial crisis of 1875, he lost both his studio and his negatives to a creditor, whose partner, T.W. Taber, soon began marketing Watkins' stereographs under his own name.

For the next 10 years, Watkins revisited locations throughout the western states in order to establish his own 'New Series' of photographs. His effort began with new views of Yosemite, which he visited several times between 1878 and 1881. By the end of his career, he had made eight journeys to Yosemite.

Watkins' eyesight deteriorated after 1890, so that by the middle of the decade he had to be assisted by his son Collis. Then the 1906 earthquake and fire destroyed his studio along with most of his new negatives. He retired to a ranch that had been given to him by Huntington's Central Pacific, but he never truly recovered from the loss of his new work, and in 1910 he was committed to a hospital for the insane.

Watkins' photographs clearly influenced the national understanding of the West and its natural beauties. Yet, despite having produced thousands of stereographs and hundreds of prints from the mammoth plates, his originals are now quite rare. The only known examples of his work in Britain are held by the Royal Geographical Society (with IBG) and the National Library of Wales.

**ABOVE**: Commoro, chief of the Latooka, running to a battle. "I am afraid of elephants ... but of nothing else," he said.

**OPPOSITE**: Baker's impression of life in camp while he and Florence were in Africa. Their pet monkey, Wallady, is in the foreground.

# SAMUEL WHITE BAKER

## EXPLORATION OF THE NILE, 1861–65

SAMUEL WHITE BAKER (1821–93) WAS A TYPICAL VICTORIAN EXPLORER OF AFRICA:
STRONG-WILLED, SELF-RELIANT, DEMANDING AND UNCONCERNED WITH SOCIAL NORMS.
BORN INTO A WEALTHY FAMILY THAT OWNED SHIPS AND SUGAR PLANTATIONS, HE
ESCHEWED ANY EARLY EDUCATION AND DEVOTED HIMSELF TO HUNTING AND GUNS.

He married at 22 and not long afterwards moved to Ceylon (now Sri Lanka) to establish an English colony in the highlands. During the next nine years, Baker's colony overcame its early growing pains and became a successful plantation. Baker, meanwhile, earned a reputation as a big-game hunter.

In 1855, ill with fever, Baker moved back to England. Shortly thereafter, his wife died of typhus. Sending his children to her family, he spent several years working and hunting in the Balkans.

In 1859 he was in Vidin, in what is now Bulgaria, when he attended a slave auction. On the spur of the moment, he bought a beautiful, 18-year-old Transylvanian girl, Florence Barbara von Szász, who had been first orphaned and then kidnapped. She became his companion for the rest of his life.

Attracted by the big game of Africa, and the possibility of earning fame as an explorer, Baker decided to spend a year in Sudan, hunting and investigating the Blue Nile. In April 1861, he

and Florence travelled to Cairo and then up the Nile to Korosko, from where they spent a year investigating the river's Sudanese and Abyssinian tributaries.

They next moved south to Khartoum, where they waited six months for the rainy season to end. Then, in December 1862, they sailed up the Nile with three boats, 29 transport animals and 96 men. In early February 1863 they reached Gondokoro, a station for the trade in ivory and slaves. Two weeks later, they were joined by John Hanning Speke and James Augustus Grant, who were returning from their own investigation of Lake Victoria and the Nile. Baker had secretly hoped to search for the sources of the White Nile himself, so he was elated when Speke told him that they had not followed its full course and that the section they missed included a large lake. Speke gave Baker a map based on what he had been told.

In March Baker and Florence moved on, overcoming the opposition of the local slave traders, who feared they were British spies. In the next nine months, they progressed only 150 miles (240 km) to the south, delayed by multiple causes: having to put down a mutiny among their men, seeing their baggage animals die, running out of food, and being laid low by fever numerous times. They then spent weeks at Kisuna, where the local king told Baker he could leave only if Florence was left behind. At that point

Baker drew a pistol and threatened the king, who quickly decided she could depart as well.

In March 1864, the party arrived at a great lake, which Baker named the Albert Nyanza (Lake Albert) after the late Prince Consort. They sailed to the point where, coming down a great waterfall that Baker named the Murchison Falls, the waters of the Nile poured into the lake. They also discovered the point where they flowed out to the north.

Making their way back north, Baker and Florence were detained again in Kisuna for six months. Finally leaving in November 1864 with a caravan, they reached Gondokoro in March 1865 to find they were presumed dead. They then made their way back to England, where Baker received the Founder's Medal of the Royal Geographical Society and was knighted. In November that year, Baker and Florence were married.

The discovery of the Albert Nyanza was the highlight of the Bakers' career, although they did return in 1869, when the Khedive of Egypt appointed Baker governor-general of the upper Nile. He went on to annex southern Sudan to Egypt under the name Equatoria, to establish Egyptian authority as far south as Gondokoro, and to attempt to suppress the slave trade. He and his wife finally left sub-Saharan Africa for good in 1873.

**OPPOSITE:** Baker was riveted by the Obbo war dance, writing they were painted, "with red ochre and white pipe-clay; their heads adorned with cowrie-shells, surmounted by plumes of ostrich-feathers."

**ABOVE:** A host of animals fleeing hunters. Baker produced many colour paintings, such as those featured, which show many aspects of what he experienced on the expedition.

## BAKER'S ACCOUNT FROM HIS BOOK *THE ALBERT N'YANZA*

Early on morning of 14 March 1864, knowing that the lake he sought was nearby, Baker could wait no longer. Crossing a deep valley and ascending a hill, he saw before him the great lake that he would name Albert Nyanza:

*The glory of our prize burst suddenly upon me! ... It is impossible to describe the triumph of that moment; here was the reward for all our labour – for the years of tenacity with which we had toiled through Africa. England had won the sources of the Nile! ... I looked down upon the great inland sea lying nestled in the very heart of Africa, and thought how vainly mankind had sought these sources throughout so many ages, and reflected that I had been the humble instrument permitted to unravel this portion of the great mystery when so many greater than I had failed. I felt too serious to vent my feelings in vain cheers for victory, and I sincerely thanked God for having guided and supported us through all dangers to the good end.*

# SAMUEL BOURNE

## PHOTOGRAPHER OF INDIA, 1863–70

BORN INTO A STAFFORDSHIRE FARMING FAMILY, SAMUEL BOURNE (1834–1912) GAVE
NO INDICATIONS OF ARTISTIC GENIUS AS A CHILD. BUT AT 19 HE TOOK UP PHOTOGRAPHY
AND QUICKLY LEARNED HOW TO WORK WITH A 10 X 12 INCH (25.4 X 30.5 CM) PLATE
CAMERA, AND MASTERED THE INTRICATE WET PLATE COLLODION PROCESS OF COATING,
SENSITIZING AND DEVELOPING GLASS PLATES.

In 1855, Bourne took a position as an assistant at Moore and Robinson's Bank in Nottingham. But he began to spend all of his spare time with his camera, including taking a tour of the Lake District in 1858, displaying images from it at the Nottingham Photographic Society's annual exhibition. He developed such a reputation for his landscapes that in 1863 he left the bank and travelled to India to turn his passion into a career.

Bourne established a partnership with the Calcutta (now Kolkata) photographer William Howard. The two men soon opened a new studio in Simla, which had that very year been adopted as the summer capital of the government by John Lawrence, the Viceroy of India. The flood of British administrators and their entourages into the town gave the two photographers a steady source of business. The next year Charles Shepherd moved his studio from Agra, and merged it into Howard, Shepherd & Bourne. In 1865, Howard left, and the studio became Bourne

**OPPOSITE**: The Taj Mahal in Agra: the ivory-white marble mausoleum built by the Mughal emperor Shah Jahan in memory of his favourite wife.

**BELOW**: A group of former "Thugs", members of an age-old organization of robbers and assassins devoted to the goddess Kali.

& Shepherd. This soon established itself as the most successful photographic studio in India.

From the beginning, Bourne & Shepherd had an effective division of labour: Shepherd in charge of portraiture, printing and marketing, and Bourne travelling throughout the subcontinent, producing a high-quality portfolio of landscape and architectural images.

Bourne undertook three major photographic expeditions. The first – on which he was accompanied by 30 porters carrying his equipment – lasted from July to October 1863. He travelled 160 miles (260 km) northeast to the Sutlej River valley in the lower Himalayas. From there he continued to the Spiti Valley, a desert area high in the Himalayas and not far from the Tibetan border.

His second journey took most of 1864. Leaving Lahore in the Punjab in March, Bourne travelled northeast to Dharmsala before visiting the Himalayan hill station of Dalhousie and the ancient town of Chamba. Entering Kashmir, he spent weeks photographing the stunning scenery of that remote region before continuing to Srinagar. Bourne then headed to the Sind Valley and on to Murree in today's Pakistan. He then meandered south to

Delhi, and completed his expedition with visits to Cawnpore (now Kanpur) and Lucknow, sites of two of the major sieges during the previous decade's Indian Mutiny.

The goal of Bourne's final, six-month journey was to photograph the source of the Ganges. Leaving Simla in July 1866 in company with an English doctor, he travelled again to the Spiti Valley. When he and his companion parted ways, Bourne continued with approximately 40 porters, crossed the 18,600-foot (5,670-m) Manirung Pass, and made his way to the upper Ganges Valley, which he followed to its source at the Gangotri Glacier. According

to the *British Journal of Photography*, the result was photographs "of scenery which has never been photographed before, and amongst the boldest and most striking on the face of the globe."

Bourne's images firmly established his reputation as one of the finest outdoor photographers in the world, with a sensitive interpretation of the Indian landscape. They also guaranteed the long-term success of Bourne & Shepherd. The firm soon opened up studios in Calcutta and Bombay (now Mumbai) and came to dominate the Indian photography marketplace.

In 1867, Bourne travelled to England, where he married. He then returned to India and continued to produce dramatic photographs. In 1870, he left India for good, returning to Nottingham and establishing a cotton-doubling business with his brother-in-law. Intent on leaving commercial photography altogether, he sold his interests in Bourne & Shepherd, including his archive of approximately 2,200 glass-plate negatives. These were reprinted many times in the following 120 years, until destroyed in a fire in 1991. Today, the studio continues under the same name and in the same building where the Calcutta operation began in 1867.

**ABOVE**: The Twig Jhula bridge over the Chenab River near Kishtwar in Kashmir. Bourne took this image during his 1864 photographic expedition.

**OPPOSITE TOP**: Three women in traditional costume smoking hookahs. Bourne's photographs remain important historical sources regarding dress and behaviour in nineteenth-century India.

**OPPOSITE BOTTOM**: Simla – the summer capital of the British Raj – covered with snow during the winter. Bourne located his studio in Simla.

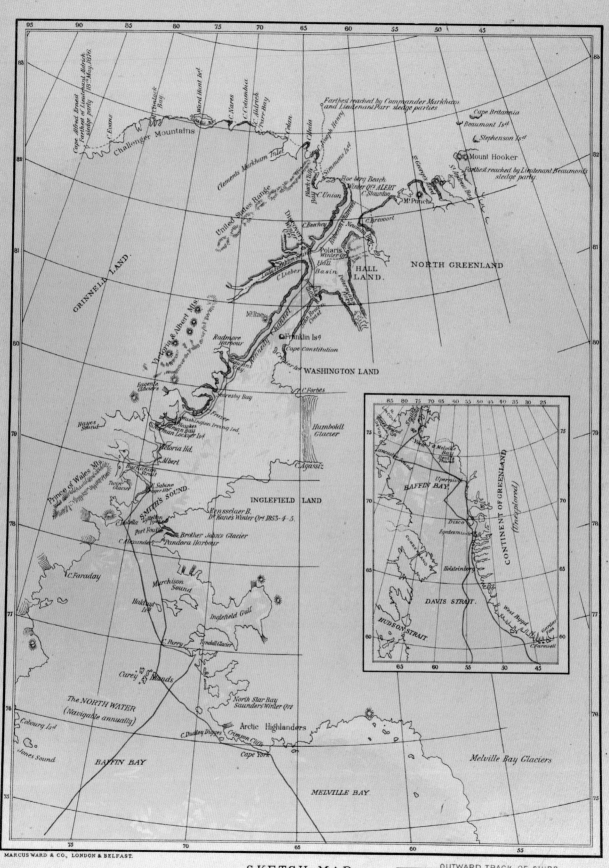

**SKETCH MAP**
OF TRACK OF EXPEDITION.

—————— OUTWARD TRACK OF SHIPS
- - - - - - - SLEDGE TRACKS
—————— HOMEWARD TRACK OF SHIPS

MARCUS WARD & CO., LONDON & BELFAST.

# BRITISH ARCTIC EXPEDITION, 1875–76

## GEORGE STRONG NARES AND EDWARD LAWTON MOSS

HALF A DECADE AFTER FRANCIS LEOPOLD MCCLINTOCK LED THE EXPEDITION (1857–59) WHICH CONFIRMED THE FATE OF SIR JOHN FRANKLIN AND HIS MISSING MEN, THE NAVAL OFFICER SHERARD OSBORN READ A PAPER TO THE ROYAL GEOGRAPHICAL SOCIETY (RGS) ADVOCATING A RENEWAL OF ARCTIC EXPLORATION.

For the next decade, Osborn and Clements Markham, the secretary of the RGS, continued to push the idea, and in 1874 Prime Minister Benjamin Disraeli sanctioned an official venture – the British Arctic Expedition.

Placed in command was Captain George Strong Nares (1831–1915), who was recalled as captain from HMS *Challenger*, then making the greatest scientific investigation of the world's oceans that had ever taken place. In May 1875, Nares' new ships – HMS *Alert* and HMS *Discovery* – departed from Portsmouth.

The ships sailed north, between Greenland and Ellesmere Island, before *Discovery* went into winter quarters off Lady Franklin Bay, northern Ellesmere. Nares continued on until stopped by solid pack ice, and at the beginning of September, *Alert* anchored at Floeberg Beach at 82°28'N, the farthest north a ship had ever reached. The sun set in October and did not return for 142 days.

When spring arrived, parties went three different ways, but the Royal Navy had made scant advances in sledging methods in the previous half century, and the massive sledges made little progress. One party went northwest along the coast of Ellesmere, charting about 250 miles (400 km) of new coast. At Cape Columbia, they reached 83°06'N, the most northerly point of land in the Canadian Arctic. However, they suffered dreadfully from scurvy and were only able to reach *Alert* on 25 June with the help of a relief party.

At the same time, a group from *Discovery* set out to explore the north coast of Greenland. Their advance was also impeded by scurvy, and half were sent back to the ship in May. The others mapped a long stretch of the Greenland coast, but on their return so many men were ill that they could not cross to Ellesmere and had to remain there waiting for rescue. They were finally relieved in August, by which time two men had died.

The final party, under Albert Hastings Markham (Clements' cousin), attempted to reach the North Pole. For the early part of the effort, they were accompanied by support groups, one under the command of surgeon Edward Lawton Moss (1843–80), who was also the expedition's primary artist.

Signs of scurvy appeared early in the journey, and they found man-hauling the sledges over high ridges of ice increasingly difficult – one day they progressed only 100 yards (90 m). On 12 May, they attained a record farthest north of 83°20'26"N, but they

---

**OPPOSITE**: Map showing the voyages of *Discovery* and *Alert* in 1875, and the journeys made by the sledging parties the next spring. The expedition proved a disappointment both to the public and in official circles.

**BELOW**: An image taken from Edward Lawton Moss's illustrated account of the British Arctic Expedition: *Shores of the Polar Sea*. In addition to the black-and-white engravings, it had 16 mounted chromolithograph plates.

BUILDING SNOW-HOUSES.

had covered a total of only 31 miles (50 km) across the ice, and by that time, only 10 of them could walk. They set off back home, still pulling a massive weight, because the supplies they had used up were more than offset by the weight of the ice that formed on their tents and sleeping bags. Their physical condition worsened alarmingly, and eventually Lieutenant Alfred Parr was sent ahead to fetch help. In an amazing display of courage and endurance, he covered the remaining 35 miles (56 km) in 24 hours. One man died before they were finally relieved.

Altogether, there had been 90 cases of scurvy and four deaths. Nares did not understand why the lime juice administered daily had not protected his men from the deficiency disease. The puzzle was solved only decades later: both the type of limes selected and the bottling process used had decreased the amount of vitamin C in the doses administered. Moreover, no lime juice had been taken on the exploratory trips, as it would freeze on the sledges.

In September, Nares terminated the expedition a year early and sailed home. It had collected impressive geological, botanical, zoological and ethnographic data, but was generally considered a disappointment due to the failure reach the Pole.

EXAMINING THERMOMETER: −73·4°.

**OPPOSITE TOP:** Another image from *Shores of the Polar Sea*, showing two members of the expedition taking a thermometer reading.

**OPPOSITE BELOW:** Moss depicts the brutal conditions in sledging north over rough sea ice. With extremely heavy sledges, the men never had a chance at real progress, and travelled only 31 miles (50 km) over the ice.

**RIGHT:** Foulke Fiord was the home of the settlement Etah, which served as base for Robert E. Peary's North Pole expeditions. Farther up the fjord was Brother John's Glacier and, beyond that, the "inland ice".

**BELOW:** From the heights of Cape Rawson on northern Ellesmere Island, one could see *Alert* anchored at Floeberg Beach, and beyond that the "Polar Sea".

# BENJAMIN SIMPSON

## SECOND AFGHAN WAR, 1878-80

LIKE RUPERT KIRK BEFORE HIM, BENJAMIN SIMPSON (1831-1923) WAS A SURGEON IN THE INDIAN MEDICAL SERVICE AND ALSO A GIFTED ARTIST – THOUGH HIS TALENT LAY IN PHOTOGRAPHY. BORN IN CLONTARF, DUBLIN, SIMPSON RECEIVED HIS INITIAL MEDICAL EDUCATION AT TRINITY COLLEGE AND JOINED THE INDIAN MEDICAL SERVICE AS ASSISTANT SURGEON IN 1853, THE YEAR HE RECEIVED HIS MD FROM THE UNIVERSITY OF ST ANDREWS.

Most of Simpson's career was spent in Bengal, where his two primary leisure pursuits were big-game hunting and photography. A member of the Bengal Photographic Society, he early on produced a set of 80 images entitled "Racial Types of Northern India". This collection was exhibited at the Great London Exposition in 1862, where it was awarded a gold medal.

In 1863, Simpson was placed in charge of the medical staff for the diplomatic mission sent to Bhutan under Ashley Eden. The Indian demands were not met, leading to the five-month Bhutan War, following which Bhutan ceded certain territories to the British East India Company.

Simpson was assigned to the Northeast Frontier in 1867–68, and he used the opportunity to take photographs throughout Assam. These images were later used to illustrate Edward Dalton's *Descriptive Ethnology of Bengal*. Some of his other pictures were used for the eight volumes of *The People of India: a Series of Photographic Illustrations*, which was published between 1868 and 1875 by the India Museum in London, and was the first large-scale ethnographic publication to employ photographs as a major element.

**OPPOSITE**: A ruined building used as a British signal tower in Kandahar. Signals were usually by heliograph, transmitting Morse Code by sunlight flashing on mirrors.

**BELOW**: Topkhana Square at Kandahar, taken over by British artillery. In the background is the Citadel, the British headquarters during the earlier Afghan siege.

In 1878, "the Great Game" was at its height, and the British and Russian empires were vying for supremacy in Central Asia. So when Sher Ali Khan, the Emir of Afghanistan, received a Russian diplomatic mission in Kabul, the British demanded that he see a British mission as well. Khan refused and ordered that a party sent by Lord Lytton, the Viceroy of India, be turned back at the eastern entrance of the Khyber Pass. In response to this insult, a British force of some 50,000 invaded and quickly overwhelmed initial resistance. However, the Afghans then initiated a series of uprisings, which were not quelled until Major General Sir Frederick Roberts defeated the main Afghan force at the Battle of Kandahar in July 1880. A treaty was thereupon confirmed that relinquished control of Afghan foreign affairs to Britain.

Simpson participated in this action, which became known as the Second Afghan War. During the previous decade the army had finally recognized the benefits of photography in field operations. Not only did it serve as a historical record, but it also offered tactical or strategic advantages: as John Spiller, the official photographer at the Royal Military Academy, Woolwich, wrote, photography was "a ready means of recording the geography and military features of a country".

Thus, as well as his medical duties, Simpson was one of the British army's primary photographers, taking about a third of the official photographs of the campaign. The professional photographer John Burke (1843–1900) also took approximately a third, and the remaining third was divided among several other photographers. Because Simpson's photographs were often grouped with these, many cannot be attributed with certainty. Nevertheless, based on those that are definitely Simpson's, it is clear that many of his best photographs came from his time in Kandahar in 1880. Most of these were marketed by Bourne & Shepherd, India's most successful photography studio.

In early 1881, Simpson was promoted to deputy surgeon-general in Southern Afghanistan, following which he was posted to the Quetta Division as the principal medical officer. He was later named surgeon-general of the Punjab and then Bengal, and in 1885 he became surgeon-general and sanitary commissioner for the Government of India, making him the head of the entire Indian Medical Service. He was knighted in 1887 and retired from the Medical Service in 1890, having served for 37 years. He continued to take photographs throughout his tenure in India.

**ABOVE:** In the background are the ruins of the old Kandahar citadel, which was destroyed in 1738 by the forces of Nader Shad. The fortress is in similar condition today.

**RIGHT:** The residence of Colonel Oliver St John, the chief political officer to the Kandahar Field Force and later the resident in Kandahar. He took part in the Battle of Maiwand, one of the principal battles of the Second Afghan War.

**OPPOSITE:** From a distance, the tomb of Ahmed Shah Durrani, who is regarded as the founder of the state of Afghanistan. In the eighteenth century, he laid the foundations of modern Kandahar and made it his capital.

# HARRY HAMILTON JOHNSTON

## AFRICAN EXPLORER AND COLONIAL ADMINISTRATOR, 1882–1901

BORN IN LONDON, HENRY HAMILTON JOHNSTON (1858–1927) HAD AN EARLY EDUCATION
THAT PREPARED HIM REMARKABLY WELL FOR LIFE AS AN EXPLORER AND ADMINISTRATOR IN
AFRICA. HIS PRECOCIOUS ARTISTIC TALENTS WERE ENCOURAGED WHEN HE WAS SENT AT THE
AGE OF 10 TO THE LAMBETH SCHOOL OF ART TO IMPROVE HIS DRAWING AND PAINTING.

He also had a regular programme of studying birds and other wildlife at the London Zoological Gardens. And from a young age he learned French, Italian, Spanish and Portuguese.

When still in his teens, Johnston made painting excursions to France and Spain, and in 1879–80 he spent eight months in Tunis, painting and adding Arabic to his languages. He also published illustrated articles in *The Graphic* and *The Globe*, including reports of French preparations to invade Tunisia – an event that led him to devote his career to the extension of the British Empire.

In 1882–83, Johnston gained his first sub-Saharan experience when he joined an expedition to Angola as naturalist, artist and Portuguese interpreter. He then travelled on his own to the Congo, where he was befriended by Henry Morton Stanley, the representative in the Congo Free State of Leopold II. Stanley was instrumental in enabling Johnston to travel up the Congo River some 250 miles (400 km), compiling botanical, entomological and avian collections as well as a vocabulary of Bantu dialects.

Johnston's subsequent expedition account convinced the Royal Society and the British Association for the Advancement of Science to place him in command of a scientific expedition to Mount Kilimanjaro. This venture introduced him to powerful figures in the Foreign Office, and led to his appointment as vice-consul for both the British Protectorate of the Oil Rivers (in modern Nigeria) and the adjoining German-held Cameroon. Johnston remained in West Africa for two and a half years, compiling extensive natural history collections and sending back a series of reports which so impressed Lord Salisbury, the Prime Minister, that he was retained as a special advisor.

In early 1889, Johnston became consul to Mozambique, a position that meant conducting official negotiations with the Portuguese about precise boundaries in southern Africa, and secretly making treaties with the chiefs controlling the areas

**ABOVE:** Johnston's painting of a selection of swamp and river animals to be found in the River Gambia. The image dates from the early part of his government service, which he spent in West Africa.

**OPPOSITE:** On climbing Mount Kilimanjaro, Johnston noted: "I came to an awe-inspiring region of immense clouds, heard the thunder bellow at me from their midst as though I had indeed disturbed and angered the God whom the natives believed to dwell in these icy solitudes."

between Mozambique and Angola. He also travelled up the Zambezi and Shire rivers to establish agreements with the Arab traders who dominated those regions. He was a stubborn man and unyielding at times, but his language gifts made him a natural for this task; he eventually spoke more than 30 African languages. The areas thus falling under British influence as a result of these treaties were divided in two – areas that would become Northern Rhodesia fell into the political sphere of Cecil Rhodes' British South Africa Company, whereas those that would become Malawi were maintained under the British government.

The following five years saw Johnston's imperial efforts at their height, as he worked to establish a British colony running "from Cape to Cairo" – an expression that, although often associated with Rhodes, was first used by Johnston in a letter to *The Times*. There was more to expanding the Empire than signing treaties, however. He believed wholeheartedly in comprehending everything possible about a region – its topography and geography, agricultural and mineral potential, flora and fauna, and human demographics. Only when a place could be thoroughly described and mapped could it be understood and thus completely integrated into the Empire. He therefore believed that geography should be "a compulsory

subject for all aspiring politicians, diplomats, and civil servants."

Johnston's hopes for a British domain the length of Africa received a blow in 1890, when a treaty ceded several slices of territory to Germany. In February the next year he was appointed commissioner and consul-general for the British territories north of the Zambezi. In this post he established a military force consisting of Zanzibaris and of Sikhs from the Punjab, and in the next several years he put down several armed attempts by local peoples to oppose British control. At the same time, he demonstrated a remarkably progressive viewpoint that emphasized educating and training Africans, so that they could benefit from the modern economy rather than being exploited by Europeans.

In 1896, Johnston was knighted. But the same year he had to withdraw from his post due to an attack of blackwater fever, which required an extensive recovery period away from the tropics. It was 1899 before he returned as special commissioner to Uganda. During his two years there, he obtained and sent back to scientists in London the first known specimen of the okapi, which was given a scientific name in his honour (*Okapia johnstoni*). As he had throughout his career, he again compiled large natural-history collections and produced an extensive photographic record. He also made one of the first two Edison cylinder recordings in Africa (the other he did in Nyasaland), capturing traditional dances and ceremonies.

At the end of his Uganda assignment, Johnson was awarded a GCMG, an honorary doctorate by the University of Cambridge, and the Founder's Medal of the Royal Geographical Society. He did not serve again on a government assignment.

**OPPOSITE**: Masai warriors from the Gwas' Ngishu (now Uasin Gishu) plateau region of Kenya. About three years after Johnston took this photograph, the area was proposed as a Jewish homeland under the British Uganda Scheme.

**BELOW**: Kavirondo fisherwomen from the region of Kisumu in Kenya. They made their living by catching fish in the northeast reaches of Lake Victoria.

Johnston unsuccessfully stood for Parliament in both 1903 and 1906. In 1908–09 he travelled to the United States and the Caribbean to make a comparative study of indigenous Africans with those of African descent. A confirmed Social Darwinist, he tended to look down on and take a paternalistic view towards Africans, but his many encounters with distinguished people of African descent changed his perceptions. His later writings showed a much greater emphasis on treating all peoples as equals, regardless of race.

Johnston spent his last two decades writing prolifically. Perhaps his most significant book was his two-volume *Comparative Study of the Bantu and Semi-Bantu Languages*, in which he classified, analysed and interpreted word equivalents from about 300 languages and dialects. During his career, he also discovered and documented more than 100 new birds, reptiles, insects and mammals, most of which he illustrated in pen and ink, charcoal, oil and watercolour.

**ABOVE:** Cane peddlers in Cuba. Johnston's travels through the Caribbean in 1908–09 took him from Cuba to Haiti, Santo Domingo, and finally Jamaica.

**RIGHT:** A well-to-do Haitian farmer. This was one of the individuals whose success led to a change in Johnston's racial perceptions.

**OPPOSITE:** The entrance to a Haitian vodou (or voodoo) shrine. The practice had its beginnings in West Africa, and came to the New World with the slave trade.

# ALFRED MAUDSLAY

## ARCHAEOLOGIST IN CENTRAL AMERICA, 1880-94

ALFRED PERCIVAL MAUDSLAY WAS BORN INTO A WEALTHY ENGINEERING FAMILY – HIS
GRANDFATHER IS CONSIDERED THE "FATHER OF MACHINE TOOL TECHNOLOGY". HE WAS
EDUCATED AT HARROW AND TRINITY HALL, CAMBRIDGE, AND AFTER GRADUATING WITH A DEGREE
IN NATURAL SCIENCES, HE TRAVELLED TO SOUTH AMERICA TO STUDY BIRDS. THERE HE FOUND
HIMSELF FASCINATED BY THE STRANGE STONE RUINS BEING EXCAVATED IN THE RAIN FORESTS.

He returned to Cambridge to enrol in medical school, but severe bronchitis forced him to abandon his studies and move to a warmer climate.

Accordingly, Maudslay took a position as private secretary to the governor of Trinidad, and moved with him when he was transferred to Queensland. In 1875, Maudslay was assigned to the staff of Sir Arthur Gordon, the governor of Fiji, and in the following five years he held several posts, including consul in Tonga and Samoa. Maudslay and Gordon both began to collect ethnographic artefacts, which later formed the basis of the University of Cambridge's Museum of General and Local Archaeology (now the Museum of Archaeology and Anthropology).

In 1880, having decided to pursue his growing love of archaeology, Maudslay left the diplomatic service. At the recommendation of ornithologist Osbert Salvin, he travelled to Guatemala and Honduras to see the Mayan ruins at Quirigua and Copan. While at Quirigua, Maudslay pulled moss from some heavily covered stones, and to his delight found hieroglyphs and designs carved in relief. He realized at once that recording them was of great cultural significance, so, having already established himself as a talented photographer, he set himself to the task. He hired labourers to chop away trees, brush and creepers to clear these hidden structures. In this way, he was able to survey,

**OPPOSITE:** The Parroquia de Santa Prisca y San Sebastían dominates the Mexican city of Taxco. Maudslay likely took this photograph while living in San Angel, a small town now part of Mexico City.

**RIGHT:** A stone carving at Quirigua, Guatemala. In 1881, Maudslay employed Gorgonio López to clear the growth away from Quirigua's monuments so that upon his arrival Maudslay could immediately start his archaeological work.

document and photograph sites not previously investigated at both Quirigua and the ruins of the ancient city of Tikal.

The most unpleasant part of the process was travelling from site to site through jungle and across ferry-less rivers, transporting himself and a vast amount of camera equipment and developing chemicals on mules. On one particularly memorable night, he noted in his journal that he was being bitten by "fleas, mosquitoes, sandflies, horseflies, *garrapatas* [ticks], and every other sort of noxious insect."

Maudslay returned to London, having realized that photography alone could not make a complete record of the inscriptions and other carved details. He now employed an expert in plaster moulding and, with four tons of plaster of Paris, returned to Guatemala in 1883 on the first of six major expeditions. Plaster casts were made of numerous hieroglyphic inscriptions, and papier-mâché casts of larger sculptures. Combined with his photography and maps, these allowed a comprehensive record and site-plan to be made for the ruins at Quirigua, Copan, Tikal, Palenque, and Chichen Itza – as well as Yaxchilan, which Maudslay was the first to describe.

He eventually published his findings in five volumes, as part of the 63-volume *Biologia Centrali-Americana*, edited in part by

Salvin. His efforts provided the groundwork for future scholars of the Mayas and helped lay the foundation that finally enabled their language to be deciphered a century later.

Many of Maudslay's original prints were put on display at the World's Columbian Exposition in Chicago in 1893, and were thereafter purchased by the founding curators of the Brooklyn Museum. Having gained official permission to do so, he also brought to London a number of outstanding sculptures from Copan. In 1922 these were exhibited on a landing at the British Museum that was given his name – the only time an exhibition area in that museum has ever been named for a living person.

Maudslay married in 1892, and he and his wife later lived for several years near Mexico City, where he photographed the daily life of the local peoples. Moving thereafter to Herefordshire, he spent nearly a decade translating the manuscript of Bernal Diaz del Castillo, a Spanish conquistador. The five-volume work was published by the Hakluyt Society.

**LEFT:** Maudslay in a Mayan building at Chichen Itza in 1889. He had the rare experience of being able to live and work inside a building that he was documenting and recording.

**OPPOSITE TOP:** A group of locals clustered on the steps of the cabildo (council) building in Santiago Atitlán, a town situated next to Lake Atitlán in Guatemala.

**OPPOSITE BOTTOM:** The Temple of Tikal from the southwest. The 154-foot (47-m) temple is so covered and overgrown with vegetation that it appears to be a much smaller ruin atop a hillock.

## MAUDSLAY'S ACCOUNT FROM HIS BOOK *A GLIMPSE AT GUATEMALA*

Maudslay was respected by large segments of the indigenous population of Central America, not so much for his archaeological triumphs, but for the way he interacted with and treated them. His fame spread far and wide after he helped save a local man's sight at Copan in 1885. As he later recalled:

*The case that brought me fame was that of a poor fellow, a blacksmith by trade, living some twelve or fourteen leagues away, who came into camp one morning with his eyes in the most dreadful state of inflammation. He told me that about ten days before, when working at his forge, a hot spark from the metal had flown into his eyes, and that during the following week every one in his village had tried in turn to get the speck out of his eye and that each one had failed. Then he heard of my arrival at the ruins, and had walked over to ask me to help him.*

Maudslay explained that he was not a doctor, but it was to no avail, and the man and many of Maudslay's workers begged him to help. That evening:

*I examined the eye with a magnifying-glass. I could clearly see a minute, almost transparent particle just on the outer rim of the iris, but the camel's-hair brush which I passed over it failed to move it. Then I screwed up my courage ... and tried to remove the particle with the fine point of a knife. The first attempt failed but did no damage, and on the second trial I got the point of the knife under the particle and it came away. By the next morning ... the sight of the eye appeared to be almost normal ... I have no doubt that he spread my fame abroad on the journey [home].*

# GERTRUDE BELL

## ARCHAEOLOGIST AND TRAVELLER IN THE NEAR EAST, 1892–1926

GERTRUDE BELL WAS BORN IN 1868 INTO A WEALTHY FAMILY THAT PROVIDED HER WITH AN ENLIGHTENED EDUCATION AND FUNDS FOR TRAVEL. MORE IMPORTANTLY, HOWEVER, SHE WAS BLESSED WITH A BRILLIANT MIND, AN INNER STRENGTH, AN OUTSTANDING WORK ETHIC AND IMPRESSIVE PHYSICAL ABILITIES. ENTERING LADY MARGARET HALL, OXFORD, AT THE AGE OF 17, SHE GAINED A FIRST IN MODERN HISTORY AFTER ONLY TWO YEARS.

Shortly after graduating, Bell began what would prove to be a life-long series of travels, venturing to Bucharest and Constantinople. A couple of years later, she spent an extended period of time in Tehran, where her step-aunt's husband, Sir Frank Lascelles, was minister to Persia. There, she studied Farsi, and upon her return published her first book, a series of travel sketches. Throughout the 1890s, Bell travelled extensively with her family, and beginning in the latter part of the decade undertook a series of expeditions in the Alps, which culminated in her successful ascent of the Matterhorn in 1904.

However, the journey that most shaped Bell's future came in 1900, when she visited Jerusalem. She studied Arabic, and from there travelled on horseback to Petra, Palmyra and Baalbek. This stimulated a lasting interest in Syrian and Middle Eastern archaeology. Five years later, she returned to Jerusalem and travelled through the Syrian deserts to Anatolia, studying the region's Byzantine churches. She later produced both scholarly and popular accounts of the journeys.

In December 1906, she resumed her research in Anatolia, after which she joined archaeologist Sir William Ramsey to study ancient Hittite sites in Turkey. Her most significant exploratory expedition took place in 1909, when she travelled from Aleppo to the fortress of Al-Ukhaidir in Iraq. This took her through territory previously uncrossed by Europeans. She returned via Baghdad and Mosul. Her account of the expedition gave an in-depth look at changes taking place in the Arabian provinces of the Ottoman Empire.

In June 1913, Bell was elected a Fellow of the Royal Geographical Society (RGS), shortly after membership was opened to women. Six months later, she began a journey into the deserts of northern Arabia, where only one Western woman – Lady Anne Blunt – had ever travelled before. She began in Damascus, where she purchased 20 camels, hired five servants and set out in secret,

**ABOVE:** Part of the guest house where Bell was confined in Ha'il. Learning that three al-Rashid emirs had been killed by family members in eight years, she noted that in Ha'il, "murder is like the spilling of milk".

**OPPOSITE:** A tower tomb near the village of Serrin, northeast of Aleppo in Syria. On her 1909 expedition, Bell travelled to the Euphrates River in what is now northwest Iraq and followed it to Baghdad.

knowing that neither the British nor Turkish authorities would allow her proposed itinerary. She travelled southwest to Amman before crossing the Nefud desert and reaching Ha'il, the ancestral seat of the al-Rashid, in February 1914. Ibn Rashid was absent from the city, and although Bell was placed in a house officially reserved for important visitors, the unfavourable response of the local clerics meant she did not have the freedom of the city and was essentially confined there for her entire stay. Despite her determination, it became obvious that the war between the al-Rashid and Ibn Saud would prevent her from continuing in the direction she wished, so she headed instead for Baghdad. From there, she returned to Britain via Palmyra and Damascus. She was later awarded the Founder's Medal of the RGS for the journey.

In autumn 1915, Bell travelled to Cairo, where she joined the military department that would become known as the Arab Bureau. The next year she joined the staff of Sir Percy Cox, the political officer with the Mesopotamian Expeditionary Force. When Baghdad was taken from the Turks, she was a key figure in the civil administration of the region. Cox was made British High Commissioner in Mesopotamia in 1920, and Bell was named Oriental Secretary. It was a position of significant power, for it meant serving as key advisor to him and also to a number of new Iraqi ministers. She continued in this position until her death.

Bell also played an important role in securing the throne of Iraq for Feisal bin Hussein in 1921. As a close advisor to the king, she became known widely as the Khatun, or Lady of the Court. After her death in 1926 from an overdose of sedatives, Bell was commemorated as a brilliant intellect who had helped to shape the post-war Middle East.

**ABOVE**: Kalaat Ja'Bar. The hill on which the castle stood is now an island in Lake Assad, reachable only by an artificial causeway.

**OPPOSITE TOP**: Bell's guides fill the water skins at a water hole en route to Ha'il in early 1914.

**OPPOSITE MIDDLE**: Two archaeologists working at Babylon when Bell visited the site in 1914. They are most likely Robert Koldewey and Gottfried Buddensieg.

**OPPOSITE BOTTOM**: Bell's servants struggle to pull her carriage over a tiny bridge across an equally small stream in Saudi Arabia.

## BELL'S ACCOUNT FROM HER PERSONAL DIARY

When Gertrude Bell reached Ha'il in February 1914, she was shown to a house reserved for important guests. A woman was sent to speak to her, but it was several hours before a man finally arrived to greet her:

*A tall slave came before Ibrahim and stood in the door, then he entered. He wore on his head a purple and red khuffa with a gold bound agal, was wrapped in a gold embroidered abba and carried a silver mounted sword. Heavily scented with attar of roses. His face is long and thin with a scanty beard and imperial; discoloured teeth and kohl blackened shifting eyes.*

# FRIDTJOF NANSEN

## THE DRIFT OF *FRAM*, 1893–96

IN NOVEMBER 1892, THE NORWEGIAN SCIENTIST AND EXPLORER FRIDTJOF NANSEN (1861–1930)
OUTLINED TO THE ROYAL GEOGRAPHICAL SOCIETY (RGS) AN AUDACIOUS AND CONTROVERSIAL
PLAN – A DRIFT ACROSS THE ARCTIC BASIN. THE IDEA HAD FIRST OCCURRED TO HIM EIGHT YEARS
EARLIER, AFTER RELICS FROM *JEANNETTE* – A SHIP CRUSHED IN THE ICE NORTH OF SIBERIA
WHILE TRYING TO REACH THE NORTH POLE – WERE DISCOVERED IN SOUTHWEST GREENLAND.

To Nansen, this suggested the existence of a previously unknown trans-polar current, and he theorized that if he deliberately beset a specially built ship in the ice, it would be carried clear across the Arctic Ocean.

Much of the scientific community was sceptical, believing that such a ship would be impossible to construct, and Nansen was called foolhardy and irresponsible. But he was not – rather, he was the greatest intellect and the most creative thinker in the history of polar exploration.

Nansen had first visited the Arctic in 1882, when still a zoology student. He was fascinated by the far north, and while continuing the neurological research for his doctoral thesis, he studied many aspects of Arctic travel. In 1888–89, he sprang onto the world stage when he led the first crossing of the Greenland ice cap, a deed for which he was awarded the Patron's Medal of the RGS. As was the case throughout his career, it was his innovative plans that set him apart from his predecessors. First, his party would travel on skis, which had never before been used under the conditions of the ice cap. Second, he would not start from the inhabited west coast of Greenland – the choice of all those who had tried previously, in part because heavy ice on the east coast meant that ships preferred to dock in the west. Instead, Nansen insisted that his party should begin the journey from the sparsely populated east coast. This meant that that there was no turning back – his reserve supplies were on the west coast. It also had the advantage that his party would have to cross the island only once, leaving by ship afterwards from the west.

There was some difficulty getting ashore, and the six-man party slowly ascended to the ice cap. Nansen then made technical improvements to their skis, at which point they virtually raced to the west coast. In the process, they showed that skis were effective in a variety of snow conditions. His designs for a light, flexible sledge and an innovative cooker were also great advances. In fact, both the Nansen sledge and the Nansen cooker remained standard equipment for polar explorers for decades thereafter.

This, then, was the man who ignored his doubters and proceeded to create an equally innovative ship. Designed by Colin Archer, she was named *Fram* (meaning Forward), and she was small and rounded, with sides sloping at an angle that prevented the ice from getting a firm hold on her hull. Thus, when squeezed between floes, the ship was not crushed but rather simply rose above the ice. *Fram* was also equipped with only the third marine diesel engine ever installed in a ship, and she was furnished with electric lights that could be driven by the engine, wind or hand-power.

**OPPOSITE:** Three images of various types of scientific work conducted during the period that *Fram* was frozen in the ice.

**BELOW:** Sugger, the last of Johansen's dogs on the gruelling march to a farthest north on the Arctic sea ice.

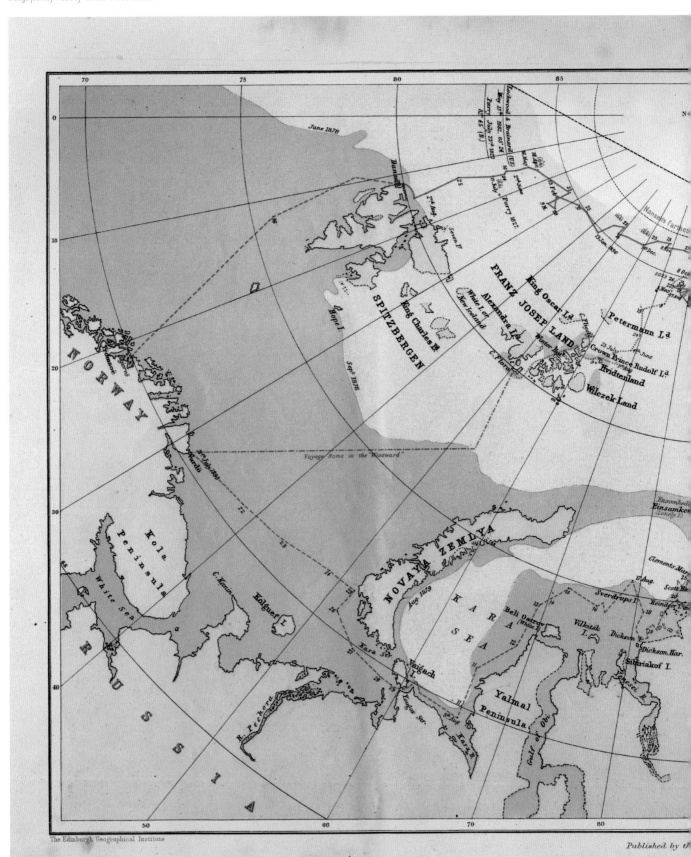

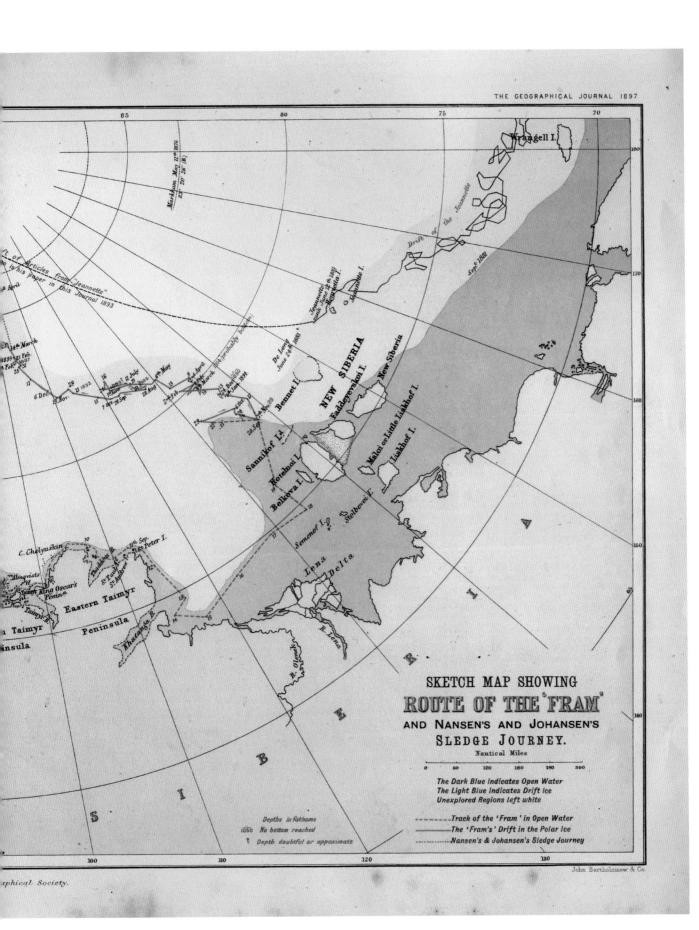

Markham May 12th 1876
83° 20' 26' (R)

Drift of the Jeannette

Sep. 1881

Wrangell I.

Tr. of Articles from "Jeannette"
to this paper in this Journal 1893

Jeannette Is. 1881
Henrietta I.

Jeannette I.

Bennet I.

De Long
June 24th 1881

NEW SIBERIA

Raddegevskoi I.

New Siberia

Sannikof Id.

Maloi or Litle Liakhof I.

Liakhof I.

Kotelnoi I.

Belkova I.

Semenof I.

Stolbovoi I.

Lena Delta

C. Chelyuskin

Almqvists

King Oscar's
Penina

Eastern Taimyr

Peninsula

Khatanga B.

R. Olenek

R. Lena

Taimyr
Peninsula

St Peter I.

SIBERIA

SKETCH MAP SHOWING
ROUTE OF THE 'FRAM'
AND NANSEN'S AND JOHANSEN'S
SLEDGE JOURNEY.

Nautical Miles

0    60    120    180    240    300

The Dark Blue indicates Open Water
The Light Blue indicates Drift Ice
Unexplored Regions left white

Depths in fathoms
1050  No bottom reached
     Depth doubtful or appoximate

- - - - - Track of the 'Fram' in Open Water
———— The 'Fram's' Drift in the Polar Ice
· · · · · Nansen's & Johansen's Sledge Journey

John Bartholomew & Co.

...phical Society.

In 1893, *Fram* sailed from Norway under the command of Otto Sverdrup, who had participated in the crossing of Greenland. After completing most of the Northeast Passage, Sverdrup entered the pack ice near the New Siberian Islands. Once frozen in, the party of 13 men and 34 dogs drifted at the will of the ice. For the next year and a half, the men conducted a comprehensive scientific programme, proving that there were no major landmasses north of the Eurasian continent and that their side of the Arctic Basin was a true, deep ocean.

However, it slowly became evident that the drift would not take *Fram* to the North Pole as hoped. Nansen therefore decided to take his greatest gamble: to make a dash for it himself, fully aware that if he left the ship in the moving ice, he would never find her again. In March 1895, he and Hjalmar Johansen, a former gymnast and army officer, headed north with 27 dogs, three sledges and two kayaks.

For almost a month the two men battled the constantly shifting sea ice, but on 9 April, having attained 86°14′N – a full 170 miles (315 km) closer to the Pole than had ever before been achieved – Nansen decided they had to retreat towards Franz Josef Land, a little-known archipelago north of Russia. They made slow progress due to the rough ice mixed with wide lanes of open water. In August, they reached land, but their chronometers had stopped at one point

and they could not measure longitude, so were they uncertain if they were in Franz Josef Land or another as-yet-undiscovered set of islands. Conditions became so bad in September that they were forced to halt and spend a long, miserable winter in a makeshift hut, living on polar bear and walrus.

Finally, in May 1896, they continued south through the archipelago. Before long, they had a remarkable, and very fortunate, meeting with Frederick Jackson, an English explorer whose North Pole expedition had made its base in the south of Franz Josef Land. After enjoying Jackson's hospitality for a period of weeks, Nansen and Johansen returned to Tromsø on his ship.

Meanwhile, *Fram* had continued her drift, reaching a high latitude of 85°55′N before being released from the ice. She finally reached land at Danskøya, off Spitsbergen. *Fram* arrived in Tromsø on 20 August 1896, just one day before Nansen, who had been proven correct in every respect and whose expedition had produced a plethora of valuable scientific results.

Nansen's return made him the darling of the international press – a role for which he was perfectly suited, being tall, photogenic, intellectual and graceful. He never led another major expedition, but his success meant that he now essentially became a polar oracle who would be consulted by virtually everyone who explored in the high Arctic or the Antarctic.

OPPOSITE: Nansen out for a walk in July 1894. While *Fram* was frozen in, the men could safely wander several miles across the ice.

ABOVE: Nansen (second from left) and Johansen (third from right) prepare to leave *Fram* on 14 March 1895 for their attempt on the North Pole. They had already made two abortive starts.

## NANSEN'S ACCOUNT FROM HIS BOOK *FARTHEST NORTH*

In early August 1895, Nansen and Johansen were desperately trying to reach Franz Josef Land on the retreat from their farthest north. After an exhausting march, they reached a lane of water where they had to ferry the sledges across on kayaks. Nansen recorded the almost disastrous events that happened next:

*I drew my sledge to the edge of the ice, and was holding it to prevent it slipping in, when I heard a scuffle behind me, and Johansen, who had just turned round to pull his sledge flush with mine, cried: "Take the gun!" I turned round and saw an enormous bear throwing itself on him, and Johansen on his back. I tried to seize my gun, which was in its case on the fore-deck, but at the same moment the kayak slipped into the water. My first thought was to throw myself into the water over the kayak and fire from there, but I recognised how risky it would be. I began to pull the kayak, with its heavy cargo, on to the high edge of the ice again as quickly as I could, and was on my knees pulling and tugging to get at my gun. I had no time to look round and see what was going on behind me, when I heard Johansen quietly say: "You must look sharp if you want to be in time." … At last I got hold of the butt-end, dragged the gun out, turned round in a sitting posture, and cocked the shot-barrel. … There was no time to lose in cocking the other barrel, so I gave it a charge of shot behind the ear, and it fell down dead between us.*

# ISABELLA BIRD

## TRAVELS TO THE FAR EAST, 1894–96

ISABELLA LUCY BIRD (1831–1904), THE DAUGHTER OF AN EVANGELICAL CHRISTIAN CURATE, WAS A FRAIL CHILD. FROM EARLY IN LIFE SHE SUFFERED SEVERE SPINAL PAIN, WHICH IN TURN LED TO FREQUENT HEADACHES AND INSOMNIA. AT THE AGE OF 18, A TUMOUR WAS REMOVED FROM NEAR HER SPINE, BUT THE PROCEDURE DID NOT ELIMINATE HER PAIN.

As fresh air was recommended for her condition, she rode horses as often as her back would allow, including on tours of the United States and Canada in 1854 and 1857. *An Englishwoman in America* was the first of a series of books she wrote about her adventures.

Bird's mother died in 1868, following which Isabella's only sister, Henrietta, moved to Mull. Although devoted to her sister, Isabella decided she could not face Mull's "unendurable climate". Therefore, in 1872, she began a journey that would take her to New Zealand, Australia and Hawaii. In Hawaii, she climbed Mauna Kea and Mauna Loa. But more importantly, she found that women rode astride horses rather than sidesaddle, and when she changed positions she found that she could ride anywhere pain-free. The discovery changed her life.

In 1873, hearing that the Rocky Mountains of Colorado were a haven for the sick and infirm, Bird went to the town of Estes Park, from where she made solo treks into the rugged mountains. Once, she fell in with a group of cowboys herding cattle. After a particularly hard day, "Our leader said I was a good cattle man and that he had forgotten a lady was of the party." Her experiences led her to write *A Lady's Life in the Rocky Mountains*.

While in Colorado, Bird met "Rocky Mountain Jim" Nugent, a hunter and trapper who had spent his life tangling with American Indians and wild animals – and had the scars to prove it. Despite being an outdoorsman, he was well read and urbane, and a close friendship developed between the two. Bird was smitten but took the safe emotional route by returning to Scotland, and not long thereafter Nugent was shot dead in a quarrel.

In Scotland, Bird met John Bishop, an Edinburgh surgeon who proposed to her. But ailing once again, she left for the Far East, hoping to recapture her health. Her time in Japan included a visit to the "Hairy Ainu" of Hokkaido, at that time considered "the most primitive and therefore the most interesting savages left to us". She then travelled to Hong Kong, China, Saigon, Singapore, and what is today Malaysia.

Bird's sister Henrietta died in 1880, and in her grief Isabella accepted Bishop's long-standing proposal. They were married in 1881, and the devoted doctor helped her recover from a serious depression. Bishop died five years later in his mid-forties, and

**OPPOSITE**: A ferocious-looking God of Thunder, which Bird photographed in the Lingyin Temple northwest of Hangzhou. The temple's name is generally translated as the "Temple of the Soul's Retreat".

**BELOW**: Tibetan lamas masked for a religious dance. Bird so liked this image that she selected it as the frontispiece for her book *The Yangtze Valley and Beyond* (1899), which recorded her experiences in China.

Isabella determined that her next journey would honour him by visiting medical missions. After studying medicine at St Mary's Hospital, London, she made for India, where she visited the clinics run by the Church Missionary Society and set up a hospital in her late husband's name in Srinigar.

In February 1890, Bird began her hardest challenge: in the company of Major Herbert Sawyer, an Indian army officer 21 years her junior, she left Baghdad for Tehran on a secret mission to establish a winter route between the two cities. For 45 days, they had to fight through driving snow and freezing temperatures, but they reached their goal. At that stage, so impressed was Sawyer by Bird's drive that he asked her to join an official deputation to the Bakhtiari people of southwest Persia. There, Bird treated the local people in need of medical aid – having been given a medical chest by the pharmaceutical company Burroughs Wellcome – and also assisted in Sawyer's survey work.

Bird's highly publicized travels made her a figure of consequence in geographical circles. She addressed the British Association in 1891, 1892 and 1898, and in 1892 was one of the first women admitted to the Royal Geographical Society. This was a victory of sorts, as she had previously declined to speak to the RGS, stating that "it seems scarcely consistent in a society which does not recognise the work of women to ask women to read a paper".

In January 1894, Bird left on her last great journey. From Yokohama, Japan, she travelled to Korea, where she explored the Han River and the region of Diamond Mountain (now Kumgangsan). She then was deported due to the tensions leading up to the outbreak of the Sino-Japanese War (1894–95), in which the modern Japanese army inflicted a string of defeats on the Chinese. She was sent to Mukden (now Shenyang) in Manchuria. For centuries the rulers of the Qing dynasty had attempted to keep the entire province separate from the rest of

**RIGHT**: A family that Bird visited. Throughout her time in Japan, Korea, Manchuria, Russia, and China, Bird interacted with both officials and common people. Her images provide a snapshot of the time's dress and customs.

**OPPOSITE**: Bird was fascinated by dwellings – such as this one – that resembled British terraced houses. While in Edinburgh, she became involved in schemes to draw attention to the condition of that city's slums.

**BELOW**: This lovely pavilion in its bucolic setting was a site frequented by Europeans. Bird interacted with other Westerners on her Asian travels, although she only occasionally sought them out deliberately.

China, limiting its settlement to the Manchus. But now, Mukden was full of Chinese soldiers. Heading south, Bird reached Peking (Beijing) before again being deported, this time to Vladivostok, in eastern Russia.

Undeterred, she returned to China, passing from Hong Kong to the Yangtze River. Purchasing a riverboat and hiring men to sail, row and drag it upstream, she made her way through the heart of China to Szechwan (now Sichuan) province. Continuing overland, she and her party were attacked several times. Once she was trapped by a mob in the top floor of a house, which was then set afire. It was only at the last minute that she was rescued by a detachment of soldiers. Finally, she crossed the Chengdu Plain to the border of Tibet. By the time she returned home, she had travelled thousands of miles – 8,000 miles (13,000 km) in China alone.

This trip was Bird's best recorded, due to her new camera and the development of her photographic skills. She brought back hundreds of pictures of Chinese life, architecture and scenery, producing arguably the best photographic record of China that had ever been made.

In 1901, Bird visited Morocco, but she remained entranced by China, and intended to make another visit. Unfortunately, she died while it was still at the planning stage.

**OPPOSITE**: A courtyard at the Church Inland Mission sanatorium in Sin-Tien. The organization was non-denominational and attempted to group missionaries together, but in that part of Szechwan they tended to be mostly Church of England.

**ABOVE**: Bird travelled by canal to Shao Hsing (Shaoxing), where she saw this temple entrance. "I made that journey without companion or servant, trusting entirely to the goodwill of Chinese boatmen, and was not disappointed."

**BELOW**: Most of Bird's photographs were taken during fair weather, but this winter image is one of her most evocative.

## BIRD'S ACCOUNT FROM HER BOOK *THE YANGTZE VALLEY AND BEYOND*

During her expedition up the Yangtze River, Bird arrived at Liang-Shan Hsien to find the local populace in an uproar – yelling, throwing sticks and mud at her, and even one well-dressed man striking her "a smart whack across my chest, which left a weal". Dashing into an inn, she was hurried to the top of the building and showed into a dark room. But a frenzied mob, numbering about 1,500, began pounding on her door, yelling: "Kill her" and "Burn her". Then, after breaking a hole in a wall:

*They inserted some lighted matches, which fell on some straw and lighted it. It was damp, and I easily trod it out, and dragged a board over the hole. The place was all but pitch-dark, and was full of casks, boards, and chunks of wood. The door was secured by strong wooden bars. I sat down on something in front of the door with my revolver, intending to fire at the men's legs if they got in ... [it was] darkness, no possibility of escaping, nothing of humanity to appeal to, no help, and a mob as pitiless as fiends ... They brought joists up wherewith to break in the door, and at every rush – and the rushes were made with a fiendish yell – I expected it to give way. At last the upper bar yielded, and the upper part of the door caved in a little. They doubled their efforts, and the door in another minute would have fallen in, when the joists were thrown down, and in the midst of a sudden silence there was the rush, like a swirl of autumn leaves, of many feet, and in a few minutes the yard was clear, and soldiers, who remained for the night, took up positions there.*

# AUREL STEIN

## ARCHAEOLOGIST ALONG THE SILK ROAD, 1900–15

IN JANUARY 1896, IN THE MIDDLE OF THE DREADED TAKLAMAKAN DESERT IN CHINESE TURKESTAN, THE SWEDISH EXPLORER SVEN HEDIN FOUND A MYSTERIOUS RUIN BURIED IN THE SAND. ALTHOUGH HE DID NOT HAVE TIME TO EXCAVATE THE SITE EXTENSIVELY, HIS INVESTIGATION UNEARTHED TRACES OF WOODEN HOUSES, CARVED IMAGES, WALL PAINTINGS, AND FRAGMENTS OF ANCIENT PAPER COVERED WITH WRITING.

What he had discovered was the long-lost oasis town of Dandan Oilik, and his find would, in turn, initiate an influx of archaeologists from around the world keen to search for – and often remove – the lost treasures of the Silk Road.

In the ensuing decades, internationally respected archaeologists from Germany, France, Russia, the United States, Japan and China descended on the Tarim Basin to hunt for, excavate, study and photograph the houses, works of art, clothing, manuscripts and other antiquities found there in their thousands. But the most determined and successful of all was Hungarian-born, British-naturalized Aurel Stein (1862–1943).

Stein was a college administrator in India, and an expert in early Buddhist culture. News of Hedin's findings thrilled him, and with the support of Lord Curzon, the Viceroy of India, he gained funding from the Indian government to lead an expedition to investigate this ancient Buddhist civilization in Central Asia.

In May 1900 he set out on his first expedition, and in December he reached Dandan Oilik, where, with a team of 30 labourers hired en route, he made a detailed survey. Fully uncovering 14 buildings, he found a plethora of artefacts, including leather goods, sculptures, wood and paper documents, coins and painted wall panels. He excavated several other sites as well, and at Rawak, another desert location, he found a large stupa – a mound-like structure containing many relics – and unearthed 91 huge stucco statues of Buddha or Bodhisattvas.

It was during this expedition that Stein first showed the fitness, relentlessness and willingness to engage in constant physical hardship that marked his entire career. It also set his career pattern of working without other Westerners – his expeditions consisted solely of Indian staff, hired local labourers and a succession of seven dogs, each of which was named Dash.

Stein travelled to Britain in 1901, where he learned his discoveries

had made him an international figure in the archaeological world. But although his success guaranteed funding for future expeditions, it also precipitated other archaeological expeditions to the sites he had found. When he returned to Rawak on his second expedition (1906–08), most of the large statues had already disappeared.

On that second venture, Stein extended his earlier digs before making major excavations at Lou-lan, an ancient military and commercial centre at the northeast edge of the Lop Desert. In March 1907 he arrived at the Cave of a Thousand Buddhas

**OPPOSITE:** Stein's party, including pack camels, in the middle of the Taklamakan, which he crossed in part on each of his three major expeditions.

**BELOW:** Kirghiz families with felt tents near Muztagh-Ata in the Pamirs. Stein led them in an attempt to climb the mountain in 1900.

(now known as the Mogao Caves), which lies near Dunhuang, a city on the Silk Road. Discovering that there was a mountain of texts, paintings and textiles hidden behind a brick wall in one of the caves, he convinced the custodian to let him view the collection. Staggered by the sheer volume – including some 40,000 scrolls, many of them dated from between the fifth and tenth centuries – he managed to obtain thousands of them in exchange for donations to the custodian's temple. Among them was a block-printed roll of the Buddhist text *The Diamond Sutra*. Dating from AD 868, it is considered the world's oldest printed book. All told, Stein acquired some 10,000 documents and scrolls for £130.

During Stein's third expedition (1913–15), he gathered so many manuscripts, frescoes, funereal bricks and textiles that it required 45 camels to transport them. As on his previous ventures, he not only brought back a remarkable volume of antiquities but carefully mapped and photographed the sites and the routes of his travels.

Stein has been called "the most prodigious combination of scholar, explorer, archaeologist and geographer of his generation". His work established without doubt the existence of a lost Graeco-Buddhist civilization that spread from India through Chinese Turkestan and along the Silk Road into China proper. The thousands of artefacts that he brought out of China can be found in many museums, libraries and archives, including the British Museum, the Victoria and Albert Museum, the National Museum in Delhi, the Sri Pratap Singh Museum in Srinigar, the British Library, the Bodleian Library, the India Office Library and the Royal Geographical Society (with IBG).

**ABOVE:** Ruins in Turfan of Buddhist cave temples from the seventh to ninth centuries AD. The region was also investigated by four German expeditions led by Stein's bitter rivals, Albert Grünwedel and Albert von Le Coq.

**OPPOSITE TOP:** A remarkably preserved body of an ancient resident of Lou-lan, which flourished for more than 800 years as a major centre of the Silk Road. The region remains extremely hot and arid.

**OPPOSITE BOTTOM:** The excavated hall of an ancient house at Niya, once a major centre on the southern branch of the Silk Road. Stein visited the site four times between 1901 and 1931.

Such holdings, so far from their place of origin, indicate why Chinese scholars and officials have long condemned him as the worst of the plunderers of their archaeological treasures. Indeed, Stein eventually had to abandon his fourth expedition to China (1930–31) due to the opposition to his work by Chinese scholars and authorities.

Nonetheless, he was honoured in the West for his work in Central Asia. Knighted, he received honorary degrees from Cambridge and Oxford, and was awarded the Founder's Medal of the RGS, as well as medals from scholarly societies in at least half a dozen countries.

Even with China off limits, he continued his work. Turning his attention to Persia, he made a series of four expeditions in 1932–36 to carry out archaeological reconnaissance, travelling great distances and making brief examinations of many areas in order to determine sites of interest for future research. He never undertook any more great excavations, but he did establish a basis for later archaeological work in the region. Afterwards, he made aerial surveys in Transjordan and Iraq, but that work was halted by the approach of the Second World War. In 1943, he travelled to Afghanistan to investigate its archaeological potential, but died in Kabul shortly after arriving.

# ROBERT FALCON SCOTT

## BRITISH NATIONAL ANTARCTIC EXPEDITION, 1901–04

THE ROYAL GEOGRAPHICAL SOCIETY (RGS) HAS GIVEN LOGISTICAL AND FINANCIAL SUPPORT TO COUNTLESS EXPEDITIONS, BUT NEVER WAS IT MORE CLOSELY INVOLVED THAN IN THE BRITISH NATIONAL ANTARCTIC EXPEDITION. THAT VENTURE WAS THE CULMINATION OF THE DREAMS OF ONE MAN – CLEMENTS MARKHAM – WHO WORKED TIRELESSLY FOR TWO DECADES FOR THE REVIVAL OF BRITISH ANTARCTIC EXPLORATION.

Markham's efforts came to fruition in the late 1890s, when first the RGS, of which he was president, and then the Royal Society agreed to support the effort. A large donation from Llewellyn Longstaff, a fellow of the RGS, was followed by a government grant of £45,000, and the proposal became a reality.

Following intense disagreements between the RGS and the Royal Society about the expedition's goals and leadership, Markham managed to shape it into his own chosen form. It would sail under the auspices of the Royal Navy, with geographical discovery as the primary purpose and science secondary. He also imposed his selection for expedition leader – a 32-year-old lieutenant from HMS *Majestic*, Robert Falcon Scott (1868–1912).

The venture began in July 1901, when the specially built ship *Discovery* sailed from London. In February 1902, having entered the Ross Sea and cruised along the Great Ice Barrier (now known as the Ross Ice Shelf), Scott established his base on Ross Island at the southern end of McMurdo Sound, on a strip of land they named Hut Point. *Discovery* was then intentionally frozen in for the winter.

There was much to learn; only one man in the team, the physicist Louis Bernacchi, had been to the Antarctic before. In the next several months, the team undertook sledge trips to familiarize themselves with their surroundings. On one, seaman George Vince lost control on a slick surface and plunged over a cliff into the sea, never to be seen again.

The winter was spent near Hut Point, with a strict social segregation between officers and crew. The scientific programme was conducted throughout, and there was much preparation for the coming sledging season. The period was also marked by lectures, theatricals and the production of the *South Polar Times*, a journal edited by Ernest Shackleton, the third officer, and illustrated primarily by Edward Wilson, the zoologist and junior surgeon.

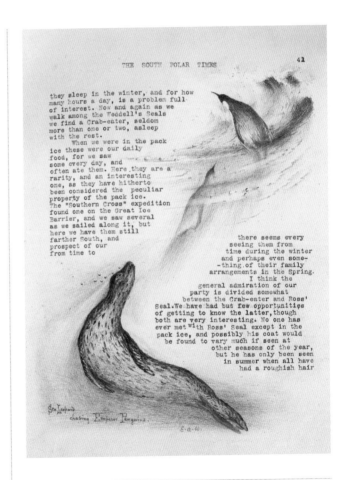

**ABOVE:** A page from the May 1902 edition of the *South Polar Times*. Wilson wrote the article on Antarctic seals and drew the sketch of a "Sea Leopard chasing Emperor Penguins". Wilson was akin to the long line of surgeon-naturalists in exploration, although he perhaps displayed greater talents as a wildlife artist. He also had a virtually unmatched ability to capture the essence and majesty of the Antarctic scenery (see page 120).

**OPPOSITE:** Cover of the April 1902 issue of the *South Polar Times*.

In the spring, following several reconnaissance journeys, Scott, Shackleton and Wilson, along with a team of dogs, headed onto the Great Ice Barrier, hoping to reach the South Pole. Unfortunately, none of them knew how to drive the dogs, and before long the three were forced to go into harness themselves and begin manhauling, a task described as the hardest work ever done by free men. For more than a month they relayed – dragging part of the load forward and then returning for the rest – thus making only one mile south for every three travelled.

The dogs began to die, and Wilson detected scurvy in Shackleton. They carried on, not halting until 30 December at 82°17'S – a record for the farthest south ever reached by man. With supplies dwindling, they turned for home, manhauling the entire way. All three now suffered from scurvy, but still they struggled on, and on 3 February 1903 they arrived at Hut Point.

Meanwhile, in November 1902, Albert Armitage, the second-in-command, had led a party across McMurdo Sound to find a route through the mountains of Victoria Land into the interior. They spent days breaking a trail up the mountains, before retreating to the Ferrar Glacier, which they then ascended. On 4 January, at an elevation of about 9,000 feet (2,740 m), Armitage's party became the first ever to attain the Polar Plateau. By now his men's health was failing, so Armitage turned back, reaching Hut Point after 52 days in the field.

Shortly after his return, the relief ship *Morning* arrived in McMurdo Sound. However, more than 8 miles (13 km) of ice separated *Discovery* from open water, and unless the weather

**OPPOSITE:** Hut Point, with *Discovery* frozen in behind the work hut, which was difficult to erect because holes for the foundations had to be dug out of frozen ground. Bernacchi stands outside one of the magnetic huts.

**RIGHT:** The crew, officers, and scientists of *Discovery* practise their skiing on an ice floe in Antarctic waters before their arrival at Hut Point. Most of the men had never skied before.

**BELOW:** Scott, Shackleton, and Wilson in November 1902, before departing on their journey onto the Great Ice Barrier. They attained a record farthest south, but struggled desperately on their return journey.

**OPPOSITE:** *Discovery*, still trapped by the ice, was joined in January 1904 by *Terra Nova* (centre) and *Morning*. Seven years later, *Terra Nova* would return to the Antarctic on Scott's last expedition.

**LEFT:** Wilson's dramatic painting of the Royal Society Range across McMurdo Sound from Ross Island. The summit of the prominent Mount Lister is 13,205 feet (4,025 m).

**BELOW:** After Wilson sketched Castle Rock, he wrote: "Though the temperature was between 20 and 30 below zero, it was so calm that I sketched for a good half hour with bare hands."

broke it up, she and most of Scott's party would be forced to winter again. When Scott returned, he and William Colbeck, master of *Morning*, agreed that the relief ship should sail north before she was trapped. Scott also decided to reduce the land party. Among those sent back was Shackleton, "invalided" home against his will.

When winter came, *Discovery*'s company settled into its previous routine, with Bernacchi becoming editor of the *South Polar Times*. Several spring journeys were planned, with the intention of everyone returning to Hut Point by mid-December, so that they could all concentrate on freeing the ship. On one of the spring treks, first officer Charles Royds, Wilson and four others travelled across Ross Island to Cape Crozier to collect emperor penguin eggs. However, they found only adults and chicks. This surprising discovery led Wilson and two companions to return to that site in the midst of the Antarctic winter on Scott's next expedition, to try to collect eggs.

Meanwhile, Scott focused on extending Armitage's discoveries. Accompanied by Reginald Skelton – the chief engineer and official photographer – and four other men, he pushed up the Ferrar Glacier and onto the barren Polar Plateau. After nine terrible days, with ferocious winds blowing constantly in their faces, Scott sent Skelton and two men back. He continued, with petty officer Edgar Evans and leading stoker Bill Lashly, but on 30 November, he ordered an about-face. With food and fuel both failing, the three raced against time to reach their depot. At one point, Scott and Evans both fell down a crevasse, and only Lashly's quick thinking and remarkable strength prevented the sledge from following them. He then helped his companions struggle out.

When Scott's party reached Hut Point on Christmas Eve, they found that 20 miles (32 km) of ice still remained between the base and the open sea. In early January 1904, *Morning* returned, accompanied by another relief ship, *Terra Nova*. Scott was told that unless *Discovery* could be freed in six weeks, she would have to be abandoned. Fortunately, most of the ice broke up, and, on 16 February, explosives were used to free *Discovery*. Scott sailed north, his return to England promising a hero's welcome.

# ROALD AMUNDSEN

## NAVIGATION OF THE NORTHWEST PASSAGE, 1903-06

FROM THE AGE OF 15, WHEN HE READ SIR JOHN FRANKLIN'S BOOKS ABOUT HIS LAND EXPEDITIONS, ROALD AMUNDSEN (1872–1928) KNEW HE WANTED TO BE A POLAR EXPLORER. BUT IT WAS ONLY IN 1893, FOLLOWING THE DEATH OF HIS MOTHER, THAT HE WAS ABLE TO CONCENTRATE ON SUCH A CAREER.

For the next four years Amundsen prepared. He made long ski journeys, joined sealing vessels in the Arctic and obtained his mate's certificate. Then in August 1897, he sailed as mate on a Belgian expedition to the Antarctic. The ship, *Belgica*, reached the islands off the Antarctic Peninsula in February 1898, and in March became trapped in the ice. Fears provoked by being the first men to experience Antarctic night (24 hours of darkness) meant that the party soon began to fall apart. But the American surgeon, Frederick Cook, instituted measures to keep the crew physically and psychologically healthy. Amundsen learned from Cook's innovations and from an extended ski trip. The next summer, the two led the successful effort to free the ship from the ice.

Returning to Norway, Amundsen next prepared for the challenge he had long dreamed about: the first navigation of the Northwest Passage. Knowing that a scientific façade was needed to gain funding, he travelled to Hamburg to study terrestrial magnetism under the famous scientist George von Neumayer. These skills would allow him to determine the current position of the North Magnetic Pole, first fixed by James Clark Ross six decades before.

In 1901, Amundsen bought a 47-ton, 29-year-old fishing sloop, *Gjøa*, which he then commanded during a five-month sealing voyage. He gained his master's certificate, and moved ahead with his plans – gaining more magnetic experience, developing his photographic skills, ordering food and equipment, quizzing previous explorers of the Northwest Passage, raising funds and taking advice from his countryman Fridtjof Nansen.

Amundsen also hired a crew of six. His party consisted of Lieutenant Godfred Hansen, the second-in-command; Peder Ristvedt, the first engineer, who had been Amundsen's sergeant during his military training; Gustav Wiik, the second engineer and a budding scientist; Anton Lund, the first officer and, at 39, the oldest man aboard; Helmer Hanssen, the second officer,

**ABOVE**: One of the Inuit families that lived near the wintering site of *Gjøa*, and had frequent interactions with expedition members. Amundsen learned an enormous amount from them that would benefit his other polar efforts.

**OPPOSITE**: *Gjøa*, the tiny fishing smack that became the first ship to navigate the Northwest Passage. Here she is anchored at Gjøahavn, King William Island, where she spent two winters.

whom Amundsen had met just before *Belgica* sailed; and Adolf Lindstrøm, the cook.

In June 1903, the expedition sailed from Christiania (now Oslo), and the next month Amundsen collected sledges, kayaks and 10 dogs in Greenland. Entering the Northwest Passage, *Gjøa* made good time initially, and they anchored at Beechey Island for magnetic observations before sailing south through Peel Sound. Keeping close to the shore of Boothia Peninsula, Amundsen's shallow-draft ship allowed him to bypass the ice that had doomed Franklin. On 12 September, they reached a sheltered bay he named Gjøahavn, where they wintered.

In October, they were visited by a group of Netsilik Inuit. In the next two years, the Inuit taught Amundsen about sledges, dog-driving, building igloos, wearing furs, and other aspects of living in the cold. Concurrently, he recorded a great deal of information about them, including a photographic record. The next spring, Amundsen and Ristvedt set out to locate the North Magnetic Pole. Their observations proved conclusively that it was not where it had been when attained by Ross; this was the first verification that the Magnetic Pole was not static.

Following Neumayer's wishes, Amundsen spent a second year in the vicinity of the Magnetic Pole – after another winter at Gjøahavn, a number of scientific and cartographic journeys were conducted. In August 1905, the expedition headed west until stopped by ice near the Mackenzie River delta, where they wintered close to several American whaling ships. That winter, Amundsen made a 500-mile (800-km) sledge trip across the Brooks Range to Eagle City, Alaska, to break the news of his successful completion of the Passage. Unfortunately, his message was leaked to the American press before it was received in Europe.

Upon his return to *Gjøa* in March 1906, Amundsen found an extremely ill Gustav Wiik, who died of undetermined causes within days. In July, the expedition was on its way again, and three months later, it reached San Francisco, having completed a journey that had been a goal of explorers for more than 400 years. Leaving *Gjøa* behind, Amundsen returned to Norway as an international hero.

**ABOVE:** The coast between King Point and Key Point. The expedition spent its third winter in the high Arctic at King Point, west of the Mackenzie River delta, finally continuing in July 1906.

**OPPOSITE:** A row of snow huts that the Inuit built in the Lindström Valley near Gjøahavn. They lived here in order to be able to barter at the ship with the Norwegians.

**TOP:** The Nechung Monastery was the home of the Chief Oracle of Tibet. The Chief Oracle currently resides with the Dalai Lama in Dharamsala, India.

**ABOVE:** White identified the man on the right as the Abbot of Kampa Dzong. Younghusband's representatives waited there several months before beginning military operations.

# BRITISH EXPEDITION TO TIBET, 1903-04

## FRANCIS YOUNGHUSBAND AND JOHN CLAUDE WHITE

THROUGHOUT MOST OF THE NINETEENTH CENTURY, THE BRITISH AND RUSSIAN EMPIRES ENGAGED IN A POLITICAL AND ECONOMIC RIVALRY FOR SUPREMACY IN CENTRAL ASIA, A CONTINUING STRATEGIC CONFLICT THAT WAS CALLED "THE GREAT GAME". FOR BRITAIN, MUCH OF THIS WAS BROUGHT ABOUT BY CONCERN OVER RUSSIAN EXPANSION, AS THE TAKEOVER OF KHANATES IN CENTRAL ASIA SEEMED TO THREATEN THE SAFETY OF THAT MOST-IMPORTANT PRIZE OF THE EMPIRE – INDIA.

Few distrusted Russian intentions more than Baron Curzon of Kedleston, the Viceroy of India. By 1903, Curzon had become convinced that the Chinese, who were the nominal rulers of Tibet, were going to turn the "Forbidden Kingdom" over to the Russians, who would then have a launching pad for an invasion of India.

After several rebuffs from the Dalai Lama, Curzon ordered the Tibet Frontier Commission to enter that country in order to establish diplomatic relations (by force, if necessary) and to resolve a dispute over the border between Tibet and the British protectorate of Sikkim. The leader of the Commission was the renowned explorer Francis Younghusband, and one of its deputy commissioners was John Claude White, the British political officer in Sikkim.

From the start, Younghusband was keen to provoke the Tibetans into a confrontation, which would allow him to turn the mission into a military venture. In December 1903, a British force numbering 3,000 entered Tibet on the pretext of Tibetan hostility at the border. Younghusband advanced to the village of Khampa Dzong, where he expected to meet Tibetan and Chinese officials.

After waiting in vain, the military column under Brigadier-General James Macdonald advanced in March 1904, going 50

**BELOW:** A photograph of the Lhasa environs, taken from the roof of the Potala Palace. The building on the steep slope opposite was the medical school.

miles (80 km) before finding the road blocked at the Guru Pass by a Tibetan force armed with antique matchlock muskets. The Tibetans refused to fight, but they would not give way either. So when a relatively minor brawl broke out, the British troops took the opportunity to open fire with Maxim guns. The Tibetans tried to flee, but the British, Sikh and Gurkha soldiers kept shooting, killing between 600 and 800.

In the aftermath of the massacre, the British pressed on to the town of Gyantse. When they reached it, the gates were open and the local garrison had already retreated. In the following months, the British continued to win skirmishes, and when the Tibetans attacked a camp, they were driven off with 160 dead to only three British casualties. Then on 6 July, the Gyantse Dzong – a heavily protected fortress defended by the country's only artillery and its premier forces – was stormed and taken. The road now lay open to the capital, Lhasa.

The force arrived at Lhasa on 3 August to find that the Dalai Lama had fled to Mongolia and that the Tibetans claimed there was no one else who could negotiate with the conquerors. Nevertheless, by the next month Younghusband had forced them to sign a treaty that allowed British trade in Tibet, required the Tibetans to pay a large indemnity (that was later reduced), recognized the border with Sikkim at a point the British desired, and forbade Tibet from having relations with any other foreign power, although Britain still accepted Chinese claims of authority over Tibet.

While much of the invasion was taking place, Younghusband had confined White – with whom he was frequently at loggerheads – to a supporting role in Sikkim. Only after most of the military action was over did White enter Tibet. At that point, his skills as a photographer – which had already been demonstrated in a remarkable portfolio from Sikkim – were shown in their best light. Using a glass-plate camera, he was able to produce perhaps the richest and most detailed pictorial account of the landscape and people of Tibet that had ever been made. He was even permitted to photograph Lhasa's monasteries, the only member of the expedition to do so. White's work has since been hailed as "certainly among the most impressive products of a tradition of quasi-amateur photography which had flourished among administrators and military personnel in India since the 1850s."

**OPPOSITE:** British tents cover the "Field of Milk" below Karo La, which is at possibly the highest altitude that a battle has ever been fought.

**BELOW:** A panorama of Lhasa and its environs. To the left is the magnificent Potala Palace, the chief residence of the Dalai Lama.

BRITISH EXPEDITION TO TIBET ••• 129

# JEAN-BAPTISTE CHARCOT
## ANTARCTIC EXPEDITIONS, 1904–07, 1908–10

IT WAS FAR FROM PRE-ORDAINED THAT JEAN-BAPTISTE CHARCOT (1867–1936)
WOULD BECOME ONE OF FRANCE'S GREATEST POLAR SCIENTISTS. HIS FATHER WAS A
RENOWNED NEUROLOGIST, WHO INTENDED THAT HIS SON FOLLOW IN HIS FOOTSTEPS.
SO, DESPITE BEING ENAMOURED OF SHIPS AND THE SEA, CHARCOT ACCEDED TO HIS
FATHER'S WISHES AND QUALIFIED AS A DOCTOR IN 1895.

Around that time, however, Charcot's parents both died, leaving him extremely wealthy, and in 1897, he abandoned medicine.

Charcot had long enjoyed short excursions at sea, but around the turn of the century he began making lengthier cruises, on which he engaged in scientific studies. He sailed around Ireland, then to the Shetland Islands, and finally, in 1902, to Iceland, the Faeroes and Jan Mayen. He soon fell in love with the Arctic, and upon his return commissioned a 245-ton, three-masted schooner, constructed for scientific research and specially designed to winter in the polar regions. The costs of the new ship – *Français* – were so high, however, that even Charcot's fortune proved insufficient, and he installed an under-powered engine that would later prove problematic.

Charcot intended his first cruise in *Français* to be to the high Arctic, but in 1903 international efforts to rescue the Swedish Antarctic expedition under Otto Nordenskjöld led him to change his destination to the Antarctic Peninsula, where he hoped to assist in the search while conducting his own scientific programme. Eventually, Nordenskjöld was relieved by an Argentine expedition, so Charcot instead forced his way through the ice west of the Peninsula, and wintered off Wandel Island (now Booth Island).

Charcot's party conducted scientific research and geographical exploration throughout the winter and spring, but

**OPPOSITE:** Two crewmen of *Français* holding giant petrels to show their huge wingspans. Charcot recorded that sometimes the petrels gorged themselves so much, they had to regurgitate in order to take off.

**RIGHT:** While climbing a peak on Wandel (now Booth) Island, Charcot and his colleagues reached a narrow breach in the rocks, which they christened *le défilé de la Hâche*, from a novel by Gustave Flaubert.

**ABOVE:** The hut on Wandel (now Booth) Island. Although it could comfortably house four men, its real purpose was to protect instruments and other valuable items in case *Français* was damaged by ice or fire.

**LEFT:** Containers of tinned food organized and stacked in ice holes in the walls of the storehouse at Wandel (now Booth) Island. The expedition members light-heartedly called the storehouse *le Grand Magasin* (the General Store).

**OPPOSITE:** A crèche of gentoo penguins. In order to allow parents to feed, one or several adults will look after a number of older chicks while the others are at sea.

when they tried to go farther south, *Français* struck a rock and began taking on water. The men worked the pumps 24 hours a day until they moved to a sheltered area where temporary repairs could be made. With her small engine faltering the whole way, *Français* just managed to reach Buenos Aires, where an inspection showed she was severely damaged. The Argentine government offered to purchase her, so Charcot agreed and returned home on a liner.

Upon reaching France, Charcot found that he was a national hero – but that his wife had divorced him, citing desertion. He soon remarried, and his scientific success garnered governmental support, which allowed him to build a larger, more powerful and better equipped ship, named *Pourquoi Pas?*.

Charcot's new expedition left Le Havre in August 1908 and reached the South Shetland Islands in December. The next month they began extending the earlier survey made of the islands west of the Peninusla. However, *Pourquoi Pas?* ran aground, tearing away sections of the hull and leaving a lower deck filled with water. Undaunted, Charcot continued south, crossing the Antarctic Circle, charting Adelaide Island and discovering Marguerite Bay, named after his second wife. They then safely settled in at Petermann Island, where scientific measurements were taken throughout the winter.

The next spring, a party set out to explore the coast of the mainland. When they returned, Charcot decided to restock his coal supply at a Norwegian base on Deception Island. While there, a diver inspected *Pourquoi Pas?* and declared her unsafe for further exploration. Charcot ignored him and returned south. He discovered a new island and named it after his father, but ice prevented the ship from coming too close, lest any further damage should sink her. After investigating as much as was safe, Charcot headed north, arriving at Rouen in June 1910.

The expedition had made significant scientific contributions, and the reports filled 28 volumes. They had also surveyed some 1,250 miles (2,000 km) of coastline, and had taken more than 3,000 photographs.

After the First World War, Charcot made regular cruises in *Pourquoi Pas?*, spending about three months each year in the Arctic, North Atlantic or Bay of Biscay. He visited Greenland in 1925, and thereafter spent much time exploring its east coast. In September 1936, *Pourquoi Pas?* was caught in a violent storm and foundered off Iceland. Charcot and all but one member of the crew were lost.

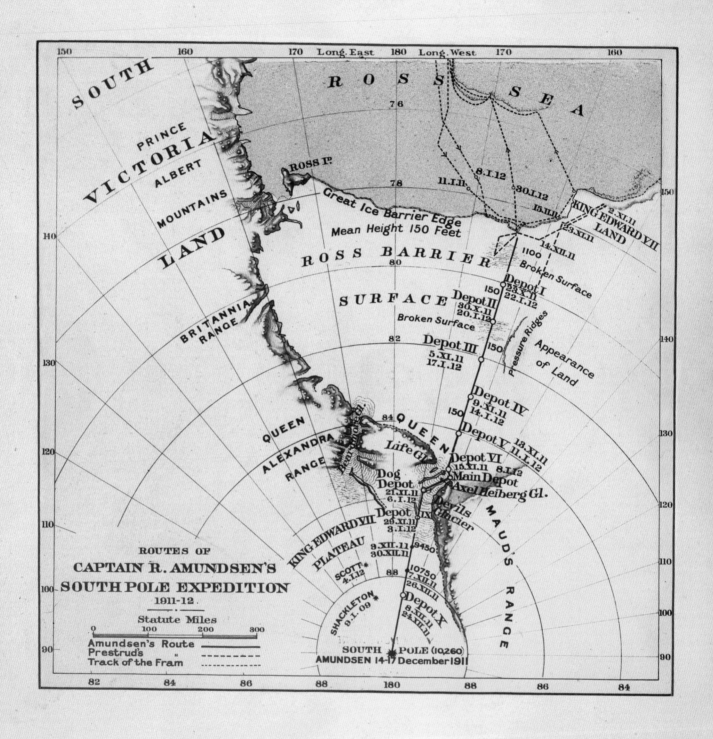

**ROSS** ... **SEA**

SOUTH

PRINCE

VICTORIA

ALBERT

MOUNTAINS

LAND

76

ROSS I<sup>D.</sup>

78

Great Ice Barrier Edge
Mean Height 150 Feet

ROSS BARRIER

80

SURFACE

Broken Surface

BRITANNIA
RANGE

82

Depot II
30.X.11
20.I.12

Depot III
5.XI.11
17.I.12

QUEEN
ALEXANDRA
RANGE

84

QUEEN

Life G<sup>L</sup>

Dog
Depot
21.XI.11
6.I.12

Depot Six.
29.XI.11
3.I.12

9.XII.11
30.XII.11

SCOTT *
4.I.12

SHACKLETON *
9.I.09

KING EDWARD VII
PLATEAU

88

Depot I
23.XI.11
22.I.12

150

150

Depot IV
9.XI.11
14.I.12

Depot V 13.XI.11
11.I.12

Depot VI
15.XI.11  8.I.12
Main Depot
Axel Heiberg Gl.

Devils Glacier

9450.

10750
7.XII.11
26.XII.11

Depot X
8.XII.11
24.XII.11

SOUTH * POLE (10260)
AMUNDSEN 14-17 December 1911

KING EDWARD VII
LAND

2.XI.11

23.XII.11

14.XII.11
1100
Broken Surface

Pressure Ridges

Appearance
of Land

MAUD'S
RANGE

8.I.12

11.I.11
30.I.12
15.II.11

**ROUTES OF**
# CAPTAIN R. AMUNDSEN'S
# SOUTH POLE EXPEDITION
### 1911-12.

**Statute Miles**

0    100    200    300

Amundsen's Route  ——————
Prestrud's      " ------------
Track of the Fram ············

Long. East   Long. West

150   160   170   180   170   160

82   84   86   88   180   88   86   84

# ROALD AMUNDSEN

## ATTAINMENT OF THE SOUTH POLE, 1910-12

SOON AFTER HIS COMPLETION OF THE NORTHWEST PASSAGE, ROALD AMUNDSEN FOCUSED ON HIS NEXT PROJECT: THE NORTH POLE. HE PLANNED TO REPEAT FRIDTJOF NANSEN'S DRIFT THROUGH THE ARCTIC BASIN IN *FRAM*, BUT STARTING FARTHER EAST. THIS, HE HOPED, WOULD TAKE HIM CLOSER TO THE POLE, WHICH HE THEREFORE EXPECTED TO REACH. BUT SEPTEMBER 1909 BROUGHT DEVASTATING NEWS.

First, Amundsen's old friend Frederick Cook announced that *he* had attained the Pole. Within days, America's most famous explorer, Robert E. Peary, claimed the same thing. Amundsen immediately lost interest in a feat that had already been accomplished. But he adjusted quickly and brilliantly, deciding instead to bag the South Pole.

Amundsen knew such a move was dangerous. The money pledged to him was for an Arctic expedition, and changing targets might mean he would lose his backing. In addition, the South Pole was Nansen's dream, and if he realized Amundsen was hijacking his goal, he might refuse use of *Fram*. That same month, Robert Falcon Scott announced his intention of reaching the South Pole, and Amundsen didn't want to be seen as an interloper. On the other hand, he believed that if he reached the Pole first, all would be forgiven.

It therefore became essential to not let anyone know his true plans. For almost a year, while Amundsen appointed expedition members, increased the number of dogs, arranged the construction of prefabricated living quarters, and gained the extra funding, he kept his secret from everyone other than his brother Leon.

In August 1910, *Fram* finally sailed, and when she reached Madeira, Amundsen told his assembled men of his change of plan and gave each the right to leave. They all remained with him. He then sent messages about his intentions to the King of Norway, Nansen and Scott.

Amundsen arrived at the Bay of Whales off the Great Ice Barrier (now known as the Ross Ice Shelf) in January 1911. There he set up his base, named Framheim, about 2 miles (3 km) inland, directly on the ice. This location put him about a degree closer to the Pole than Scott's base. Nine men were left when *Fram* returned north, and in the two months before the sun set, they established depots at 80°S, 81°S and 82°S.

**ABOVE**: Amundsen in his furs, a manner of dress for polar travel that he learned from the Inuit. His experiences in the Arctic benefited him greatly on his successful South Pole expedition.

**OPPOSITE**: Map showing the route Amundsen took across the Great Ice Barrier, up the Axel Heiberg Glacier, and over the Plateau to the South Pole.

Amundsen was anxious that Scott, with his motor sledges, should not be allowed a head start. He therefore decided to leave in early September, despite knowing it was well before the temperature would normally be at a safe level to travel. Leaving the cook, Adolf Lindstrøm, at Framheim, he and the seven others, along with 86 dogs, headed south. But it was indeed far too early, and the temperatures crashed to –69°F (–56°C), causing Helmer Hanssen, Jørgen Stubberud and Kristian Prestrud to suffer major frostbite and two of the dogs to freeze to death. Amundsen decided to depot the food and return to Framheim.

The final day of the trip back became a wild race, as the men became separated by many hours, with worsening weather threatening the lives of the slower ones. Amundsen, Hanssen and Oscar Wisting were the first to reach Framheim, Stubberud coming in two hours later with the champion skier Olav Bjaaland. Prestrud lagged far behind and might not have made it back at all had not Hjalmar Johansen – who had been Nansen's companion on his farthest north – waited hours for him on the Barrier.

The next morning, Johansen openly challenged Amundsen's decisions. There was no place, Johansen felt, for a leader who left his men and raced back to save himself. Johansen was undoubtedly correct, but no leader could allow himself to be challenged in this way, so Amundsen quashed any dissidence by dismissing Johansen from the polar party.

Instead, Johansen, Stubberud and Prestrud would travel towards the previously unreached King Edward VII Land.

**ABOVE**: Five wooden crates holding food, supplies or equipment could be hauled by one dog team. Some 900 crates were moved between *Fram* and Framheim at a rate of about 150 per day.

**BELOW**: Framheim was built right on the Great Ice Barrier. The large, 16-man tents each housed one dog team.

A month later, Amundsen and his reduced polar party again headed south, with four sledges and 54 dogs. The men with Amundsen were Bjaaland, Wisting and two experienced dog drivers: Hanssen, a companion from *Gjøa*, and Sverre Hassel. Amundsen planned to travel 15 geographical miles (27.8 km) – or one quarter of a degree – each day, thus never tiring his men or dogs. This pace also allowed the party time to build cairns to prevent them from becoming lost on their return, and to set up a transverse-marking system so that the depots could not be missed regardless of the weather.

Within two weeks they passed 82°S and began sledging through territory never seen before by human eyes. Soon thereafter, they made a remarkable four-day ascent of the Axel Heiberg Glacier, passing through the Transantarctic Mountains to the Antarctic Plateau. At 85°26'S, 24 dogs were shot, the remaining 18 being kept for the dash to the Pole.

On 8 December, the party passed Ernest Shackleton's Farthest South record of 88°23'S, set in 1909. Nervous that they might find Scott had beaten them to the Pole, they pressed on, reaching their goal on 14 December (more than a month ahead of Scott). There they planted the Norwegian flag, raised a tent, and spent several days skiing in each direction to ensure they had attained the Pole regardless of the accuracy of their measurements. Then, with depots all the way back, they made the return with relative ease, to find *Fram* waiting. Amundsen set sail north, arriving in Hobart, Tasmania on 7 March 1912, to announce his victory to the world.

## AMUNDSEN'S ACCOUNT FROM HIS PERSONAL DIARY

On 14 December 1912, Amundsen and his companions became the first men ever to stand at the South Pole. That night, he recorded the event without a great deal of emotion:

*And so at last we reached our destination and planted our flag on the geographical South Pole, King Haakon VII's plateau. Thank God! This took place at 3pm ... Of course, we are not exactly at the 90° point, but we must, according to all our excellent observations and instruments, be very near. We came here with three sledges and 17 dogs. Helmer killed one just after our arrival. "Helge" had collapsed. Tomorrow we shall go out in three directions to encircle the pole area ... We will leave here the day after tomorrow with two sledges. The third will be left here. At the same time, we shall leave a small three-man tent (Rønne) with the Norwegian flag and a flag marked "Fram".*

**BELOW:** Amundsen and Hanssen checking their position, using a sextant and an artificial horizon. The party took numerous observations around a broad area to make certain they had actually reached the South Pole.

# ROBERT FALCON SCOTT

## *TERRA NOVA* EXPEDITION, 1910–13

WHEN ERNEST SHACKLETON RETURNED FROM THE ANTARCTIC IN 1909, HE BECAME AN INSTANT HERO, IDOLIZED THE WORLD OVER FOR HIS REMARKABLE JOURNEY THAT TOOK HIM 97 GEOGRAPHICAL MILES (180 KM) FROM THE SOUTH POLE. BUT THERE WAS ONE MAN WHO WAS RELIEVED THAT SHACKLETON HAD LEFT THOSE LAST MILES UNCROSSED – HIS FORMER COMMANDER, ROBERT FALCON SCOTT.

A renowned explorer himself, Scott had led the British National Antarctic Expedition (1901–04) on which Shackleton was a junior officer. Ever since, Scott had wanted to command another Antarctic effort, and in 1907 he had approached the Royal Geographical Society (RGS) for support. Then Shackleton announced his own expedition, and for two years Scott anxiously awaited his rival's return – and the news that the Pole was still virgin territory.

On 13 September 1909, Scott made his intentions official. "The main object of this Expedition is to reach the South Pole," he wrote, "and to secure for the British Empire the honour of that achievement." Concurrently, he planned on a scientific programme that would exceed even the lauded results from his first expedition. In charge of it was his close friend and old sledging-mate Edward Wilson.

Scott's first challenge was to raise funds, a process that was excruciatingly slow until E.R.G.R. "Teddy" Evans, a naval officer who had been organizing his own expedition, joined Scott as second-in-command, bringing with him substantial financial help. That was followed by a government grant of £20,000, allowing Scott to purchase the former whaler *Terra Nova*. Finding men for the expedition was not so difficult: more than 8,000 applied. Scott selected a number from his first expedition, including petty officers Edgar Evans and Tom Crean, and chief stoker Bill Lashly. Two men won positions by contributing £1,000 each – Captain L.E.G. Oates, who was placed in charge of the expedition's ponies, and Apsley Cherry-Garrard, the assistant zoologist. Another important addition was a talented photographer and cinematographer, Herbert Ponting. Scott hoped that Ponting's photographs and film would later help pay off some of the expedition debts.

*Terra Nova* sailed from Cardiff on 15 June 1910. Four months later, she arrived at Melbourne, where Scott received a mysterious telegram: "Beg leave to inform you, *Fram* proceeding Antarctic. Amundsen." It was clearly from the Norwegian explorer Roald Amundsen, but he had been planning a drift through the Arctic basin on Fridtjof Nansen's ship *Fram*, so Scott remained uncertain of its meaning.

On 29 November, *Terra Nova* sailed south from New Zealand and directly into a violent gale that threatened to sink her. Then, as she tried to enter the Ross Sea, a belt of ice stopped her dead in her tracks. It was not until 4 January 1911 that, with the way to his

OPPOSITE: *Terra Nova* framed by the edge of an iceberg while tied to the ice foot off Cape Evans in January 1911.

BELOW: Biologist Dennis Lillie, who spent the expedition working aboard *Terra Nova*, with some of the siliceous sponges he collected in dredging operations.

original quarters at Hut Point blocked, Scott decided to establish a new base, choosing a small promontory that he named Cape Evans in honour of his second-in-command.

As soon as feasible, Scott began laying depots for the spring journey toward the Pole. At the same time, *Terra Nova* sailed east to drop a party under the command of Victor Campbell at King Edward VII Land on the far side of the Great Ice Barrier (now known as the Ross Ice Shelf). Halted by pack ice, Campbell decided to land on the Barrier. But on reaching a location that Shackleton had named the Bay of Whales, he was shocked to discover *Fram* nestling against the ice edge. Amundsen had arrived three weeks earlier and set up a base named Framheim, which was a full degree closer to the Pole than Cape Evans. Campbell hurried back to report to Scott. *Terra Nova* then sailed north, dropping off Campbell and his five men at Cape Adare, the site of the first wintering on the Antarctic continent.

Meanwhile, Scott had established several depots, although the most southerly, One Ton Depot, was some 30 geographical miles (55 km) short of his original goal. Six ponies were lost on the return journey, which led Scott to postpone his spring departure to ensure better conditions for the remaining ones. Upon arriving back at base, he received the message from Campbell confirming that Amundsen was aiming for the Pole.

The most memorable event of the winter was a journey made by Wilson, Cherry-Garrard and Henry "Birdie" Bowers to the emperor penguin colony at Cape Crozier on the far side of Ross Island. Wilson had long been keen to collect the eggs of emperor penguins in order to test theories about the origin of birds. The journey needed to be made in the dead of winter, when the emperors incubated, so in the continual dark, they hauled their two heavy sledges across the rough Barrier surface while temperatures plummeted to −77°F (−61°C). At Cape Crozier, they

**ABOVE:** Oates with the ponies in the tiny stables specially built for them aboard *Terra Nova*. The expedition took ponies of a light colour because those had lived longer than the dark ones on Shackleton's expedition.

**RIGHT:** Tom Crean and Edgar Evans mending reindeer sleeping bags during the winter of 1911. The early depot-laying on the Barrier taught the men what improvements could be made to their equipment.

**OPPOSITE:** Furling the sails while *Terra Nova* was in the ice. The men aloft are the Norwegian ski expert Tryggve Gran and able seaman Joseph Leese.

built a small igloo near the colony and gathered the eggs. Then, after a devastating gale, they slogged back the 57 miles (105 km) to base. The effort took more than a month, and was immortalized in Cherry-Garrard's book *The Worst Journey in the World*.

On 1 November 1911 – almost two weeks after Amundsen left Framheim – Scott set out for the Pole, with 10 ponies, two teams of dogs and two motor sledges under the command of Teddy Evans. Frustratingly, the expensive motorized equipment soon broke down, and Evans' party was forced to begin manhauling. In the following weeks a number of ponies wore out and were shot. Slowly Scott sent back his support personnel, and at the base of the Beardmore Glacier, the remaining ponies were put down and the dogs returned to base. Scott and his men would manhaul the rest of the way, following the route pioneered by Shackleton – ascending the Beardmore Glacier to the Polar Plateau. Once on the Plateau, Scott eventually sent Evans and the last support party back, and led a group of five onward.

On 17 January 1912, Scott, Wilson, Bowers, Oates and Edgar Evans reached what had been their cherished goal. But their excitement was tempered by the discovery that Amundsen's five-man party and their dog teams had reached the Pole on 14 December. The disheartened British explorers – already dangerously exhausted from manhauling – could do little more than take pictures and

**TOP:** Scott (centre) and some of the men involved in the attempt on the South Pole pose in front of Mount Erebus. Wilson and Bowers are seated on the sledge at the left.

**ABOVE:** Having finished their geological research, the members of the second Western Party pull their sledge over gaps between floes as they race for the ship across 2 miles (3.7 km) of ice.

dejectedly head north. "Now for the run home and a desperate struggle," wrote Scott. "I wonder if we can do it."

Tragically they could not. On the return journey of some 750 geographical miles (1,400 km), struggling against both inadequate food and fuel and worsening weather, they wore out. First, Evans died near the base of the Beardmore Glacier. Then, having sledged most of the way across the Barrier, Oates, whose feet were badly frostbitten, walked out of the tent to his death in order not to hold his companions back. But only days later, Scott, Wilson and Bowers were stopped by a fierce storm, and the three eventually weakened and died in their tent, only 11 geographical miles (20 km) short of One Ton Depot. Had this been placed where Scott had originally intended, it would have provided the food and fuel necessary to save them.

Meanwhile, the men at Cape Evans made various efforts to assist the return of the Polar Party, but were hampered not only by atrocious weather but also by a lack of clear instructions from Scott. When *Terra Nova* returned to Cape Evans to collect the entire party, she was forced to leave some the expedition members behind to wait for the Polar Party. But as winter approached, they

**ABOVE**: Herbert Ponting working in his darkroom at Cape Evans. Ponting, who referred to himself as a "camera artist", also slept in the small, confined space, which constantly smelled of photographic chemicals.

**BELOW**: At the end of winter, Ponting photographed Castle Berg, writing: "as the sun flooded it with his light, the berg became of such gleaming beauty that even the most unimpressionable members of our community felt the influence of its spell."

realized that Scott and his men would not be coming back, and there was nothing more they could do.

The men at Cape Evans were also concerned about the six members of the Northern Party. After spending the first winter at Cape Adare, they had been collected by *Terra Nova*, and left on the Victoria Land coast with supplies for a few weeks. However, heavy ice prevented the ship from reaching them again, and they were forced to cut a tiny, underground ice cave in which to winter. Suffering incredible mental and physical hardship, they somehow survived, living mainly off seals and penguins that they caught, and, beginning in late September, despite being weak and sickly, made a remarkable 37-day march to Cape Evans.

What they found there was that most of the remaining men, under the command of surgeon Edward Atkinson, had already headed south to look for the Polar Party. On 12 November 1912, they discovered the tent containing the bodies of Scott, Wilson and Bowers. They retrieved the journals, correspondence and photographs. And thus the tragic fate of Scott's party became known.

---

**ABOVE**: Scott's party at the South Pole, following the devastating discovery that Amundsen and his men had arrived there first. The five explorers are (from left): Wilson, Scott, Edgar Evans, Oates, and Bowers.

**OPPOSITE**: Map of the route of the Polar Party to the South Pole, showing where the various support parties turned back. It also marks where the members of the Polar Party died.

## SCOTT'S "MESSAGE TO THE PUBLIC"

Among the records, diaries and letters discovered by the search party in the tent where Scott, Wilson and Bowers died was Scott's Message to the Public. After mentioning the reasons for the failure of the Polar Party to return safely, Scott continued:

*For four days we have been unable to leave the tent – the gale howling about us. We are weak, writing is difficult, but for my own sake I do not regret this journey, which has shown that Englishmen can endure hardships, help one another, and meet death with as great a fortitude as ever in the past. We took risks, we knew we took them; things have come out against us, and therefore we have no cause for complaint, but bow to the will of Providence, determined still to do our best to the last. ...*

*Had we lived, I should have had a tale to tell of the hardihood, endurance, and courage of my companions which would have stirred the heart of every Englishman. These rough notes and our dead bodies must tell the tale, but surely, surely, a great rich country like ours will see that those who are dependent on us are properly provided for.*

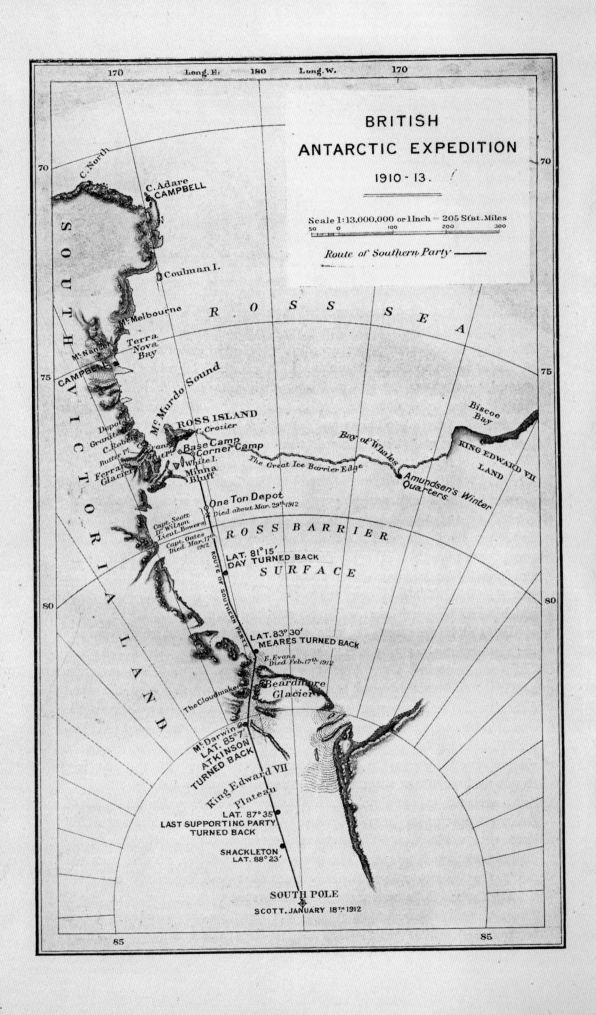

# WILLIAM SHAKESPEAR

## EXPLORATION OF ARABIA, 1909–15

WILLIAM HENRY IRVINE SHAKESPEAR WAS AN INTRIGUING COMBINATION OF PERSONALITIES. ON THE ONE HAND, HE WAS THE QUINTESSENTIAL PRE-GREAT WAR BRITISH OFFICER: WELL-SPOKEN, POISED, PERFECTLY GROOMED AND IMMACULATELY DRESSED. ON THE OTHER, HE WAS AT HEART A NOMAD, A RESTLESS LONER WHO LOVED NOTHING MORE THAN WANDERING THE EMPTY ARABIAN DESERTS.

Born in what is now Pakistan in 1878, he was educated in England and passed out of Sandhurst at the age of 19. During six years in the Indian Army, he learned Arabic, Persian, Pashto and Urdu, and in 1904, after transferring to the political service, he became the youngest Consul in British India.

One of Shakespear's greatest adventures came in 1907 on his return to Britain for his first long leave. He bought an eight-horsepower, single-cylinder Rover and despite there being no paved roads for more than three-quarters of the journey, drove to Britain from Bushehr on the Persian Gulf through Persia, Turkey, Greece, Macedonia, Montenegro, Croatia, Italy and France, making sure his white tyres were cleaned and brass lamps polished at every opportunity.

In April 1909, Shakespear was appointed the political agent in Kuwait, making him the primary British contact with its emir, Mubarak al-Sabah. He also quickly became familiar with the politics of the Arabian Peninsula, including the long struggle between the al-Rashid, whose centre of power was in Ha'il in the north, and their historic enemies, the House of Saud – with its charismatic and dynamic leader who became known as Ibn Saud.

In 1902, Ibn Saud had recaptured his family's ancestral home of Riyadh from the al-Rashid, and he thereafter continued a war against them and their Ottoman allies. When Shakespear was appointed, one of his first tasks was to report to his superiors that the young Ibn Saud sought protection like that given by the British to Mubarak.

**OPPOSITE**: A Bedouin of the Ajman tribe of northeastern Arabia travelling with a *Hawdaj*, a camel litter for women.

**BELOW:** Wadi Rum, east of Aqaba, is the largest wadi (valley) in Jordan. It is sometimes called the Valley of the Moon, and boasts many petroglyphs.

Although Shakespear's pleas fell on deaf ears, he and Ibn Saud developed a close relationship, and the political agent took the first photograph ever of the ruler. In the following years, while Ibn Saud conducted the campaign that saw him complete his conquest of the Najd (the central region of the Arabian Peninsula), he remained friends with Shakespear despite the British government continually refusing to recognize his regime.

From the time of his appointment through 1914, Shakespear made a series of journeys into the centre of Arabia, through which he came to know and understand the local peoples. Each excursion was carefully recorded by maps, photography (such as these featured images) and detailed journal entries. In January 1914, Shakespear rode from Kuwait to Riyadh to be Ibn Saud's guest. Rather than returning the same way, he headed west, travelling to the Suez Canal via Buraydah and Al Jawf. The journey of approximately 1,800 miles (2,900 km) took 111 days across previously uncharted territory.

From Egypt, Shakespear returned to Britain to convince his superiors to support Ibn Saud. He had little success until the

**ABOVE:** A Himyaritic inscription (photographed upside down) from the ancient town of Thaj, founded after the conquest by Alexander the Great in 330 BC.

**BELOW:** A large well in the garden at Shamsiyyah in March 1914. The men are sheiks of the Al-Saud family.

outbreak of the First World War, when the India Office realized the advantages of cultivating a friendly power in the Near East. Instructed to offer the long-sought alliance, Shakespear returned to Kuwait and thence continued to an area 200 miles (320 km) north of Riyadh, where Ibn Saud was on campaign.

The two friends negotiated a draft treaty, but on 24 January 1915, before it could be finalized, Ibn Saud's troops engaged al-Rashid forces at Jarrab. Shakespear, as always, refused to exchange his military uniform for local dress, so he stood out as he took photographs from a nearby ridge. When the fighting unexpectedly swung near to his position, he was shot three times and killed.

Years later the noted Arabist St John Philby suggested that Shakespear's death dramatically changed the British intervention in the Arab Revolt. Had Shakespear lived, he claimed, British support likely would have gone to Ibn Saud rather than Hussein ibn Ali, who was favoured by T.E. Lawrence. Such a change might have produced a very different set of post-war relations between the Arab world and the West.

**ABOVE:** A new-born camel is carried in a saddlebag by her mother, which immediately after the birth had to continue her journey.

**BELOW:** A midday halt for coffee by Shakespear's party in the midst of the Saudi Arabian desert.

# ERNEST SHACKLETON

## IMPERIAL TRANS-ANTARCTIC EXPEDITION, 1914–17

WHEN ROALD AMUNDSEN ANNOUNCED IN MARCH 1912 THAT HE HAD SUCCESSFULLY
REACHED THE SOUTH POLE, SIR ERNEST SHACKLETON (1874–1922) KNEW AT ONCE WHAT
HIS OWN NEXT GOAL WAS. "ANOTHER EXPEDITION UNLESS IT CROSSES THE CONTINENT
IS NOT MUCH," HE WROTE TO HIS WIFE EMILY. THEREFORE, HE WOULD LEAD "A
TRANSCONTINENTAL JOURNEY FROM SEA TO SEA, CROSSING THE POLE."

The concept was actually based on plans first formulated by Scottish oceanographer William Speirs Bruce. But Bruce had been unable to obtain funding, and in 1911 German explorer Wilhelm Filchner had headed south to cross the continent using horse-drawn sledges. Filchner's plans were ruined when a large section of the ice shelf upon which he had established his base calved off. In the process of rescuing the materials, the expedition ship, *Deutschland*, was caught in the ice. She was released only nine months later, far to the north.

Once Shackleton heard that Filchner had been unsuccessful, he began planning his own venture. He intended to use two ships. The first would land 14 men at the base of the Weddell Sea. Six would make the trans-Antarctic journey (some 1,700 miles/2,750 km) with 100 dogs and two motor sledges. They would head straight to the South Pole, then turn towards McMurdo Sound, following the route Shackleton had pioneered on his British Antarctic Expedition of 1907–09 (BAE), down the Beardmore Glacier and across the Great Ice Barrier (now known at the Ross Ice Shelf).

The second ship would go directly to McMurdo Sound, where Shackleton's hut at Cape Royds and Robert Falcon Scott's former bases at Cape Evans and Hut Point could provide accommodation. Six men with dogs and another motor sledge would then lay depots across the Barrier, for use by the group crossing the continent.

Despite some withering criticism, Shackleton moved ahead like a whirlwind in the ensuing months. With the funds he raised – the largest donation came from Sir James Caird – he purchased equipment, supplies and dogs. He also obtained two ships – *Aurora* for the Ross Sea and *Polaris* for the Weddell Sea. The latter he renamed *Endurance* in honour of his family motto: *Fortitudine Vincimus* – "By endurance we conquer."

More than 5,000 people applied to join the expedition. One of the first men Shackleton selected was Frank Wild, who had accompanied him on his farthest south journey on the BAE and was to be second-in-command. As masters of his ships, he chose New Zealander Frank Worsley for *Endurance* and Æneas Mackintosh, another old friend from the BAE, for *Aurora*. Tom Crean, who had served on Scott's expeditions, was named second officer, and Shackleton also brought aboard a large scientific staff. One of the men with the most Antarctic experience was Australian Frank Hurley, the photographer from Douglas Mawson's Australasian Antarctic Expedition.

**OPPOSITE:** Shackleton looking over the side of *Endurance*, which was hopelessly trapped in the ice of the Weddell Sea, October 1915.

**BELOW:** Map drawn by Shackleton on a menu card at a dinner in March 1914, showing the planned route for his Antarctic crossing.

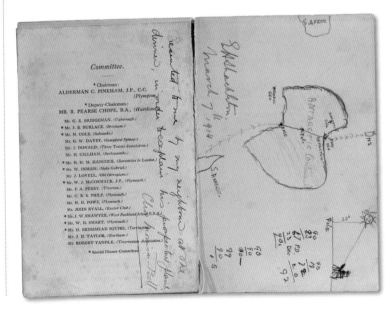

*Endurance* sailed on 1 August 1914. Before she was out of British waters, however, the Royal Navy mobilized in response to the German declaration of war on Russia. Shackleton immediately offered the ship, staff and provisions for the war effort. Winston Churchill, the First Lord of the Admiralty, instructed him to proceed south.

They reached South Georgia in early November. There, whalers recommended that Shackleton delay heading south, as the ice was unusually heavy. *Endurance* finally sailed on 5 December, but soon met the ice pack. The expedition progressed slowly through the Weddell Sea, dodging around heavy floes or battering through thinner ice. Everyone seemed on edge due to the wait, with one exception – Hurley.

"H is a marvel," Worsley wrote. "[H]e perambulates alone aloft & everywhere, in the most dangerous & slippery places he can find, content & happy."

In mid-January 1915, only a day from their destination, the pack closed tightly around the ship. The men waited for its hold to break, but it never did, and *Endurance* drifted slowly west. In the following months, *Endurance* was battered, twisted and pinched, as she was carried hundreds of miles in a clockwise direction. In October, as the approaching spring gave the men hope for escape, three converging pressure ridges virtually tore out the sternpost and caused *Endurance* to list precariously to starboard. Water poured in, and after three days of futile pumping, Shackleton gave the order to abandon ship.

Initially, the party moved about 100 yards (90 m). Several

**TOP:** "Took colour camera to lead this morning," wrote Hurley, "for a fine crop of ice flowers springing up on the lead & they, illumined by the morning sun, resembled a field of pink carnations."

**ABOVE:** Leonard Hussey, the meteorologist and the smallest man on the expedition, lifting Samson, one of the largest dogs.

**OPPOSITE:** Worsley and first officer Lionel Greenstreet high above the whaling station at Grytviken on South Georgia, with *Endurance* at anchor.

ABOVE: Wild surveys the forlorn remains of his former home. On 14 November 1915 – just a week before *Endurance* finally sank – he and Hurley walked back to the ship from Ocean Camp.

LEFT: The members of the expedition struggling under the brutal work of hauling a sledge bearing *James Caird* across the ice. When loaded, the boat weighed more than a ton.

OPPOSITE TOP: Members of the expedition were able to distract themselves from their long wait by playing football on the sea ice. Surgeon Alexander Macklin and biologist Robert Clark were considered the best players.

OPPOSITE BOTTOM: Taking a sun sighting in November 1915, after the lookout tower was erected at Ocean Camp. Soon thereafter, Hurley sealed his lenses and negatives in tin canisters and used only a vest pocket Kodak camera for taking pictures.

days later, they began hauling three lifeboats and their food and supplies over the ice, hoping to reach a hut some 300 miles (480 km) away. But three days of brutal labour saw them progress less than two 2 miles (3.2 km), so Shackleton called it quits and they set up a new base, christened Ocean Camp.

Shackleton let Hurley return to the ship for his glass-plate negatives. Hurley hacked through an inside wall of the ship and found them beneath 4 feet (1.2 m) of slushy ice. He dived in to retrieve them; having been soldered in double tin linings, they were all safe. Hurley and Shackleton then went through the 400 images, and chose to keep 120, as well as an album of developed prints. Hurley shattered the remaining negatives, so that he would not later be tempted to rethink what he picked.

A month and a half later – after *Endurance* had sunk – they began another march towards open water. Again the back-breaking work proved too much, and Harry McNish, the carpenter, refused to continue. Shackleton quelled his mutinous mutterings, but shortly thereafter ordered another halt. The party remained at what became known as Patience Camp for more than three months, while the northerly drift and the breakup of the ice continued. In early April 1916, the men spied the peaks of

Elephant Island in the distance, and Shackleton ordered the three boats launched in the nearby open water.

For the next six days the men were tormented by blustery winds, a massive swell, constant soaking by freezing water, seasickness, hunger, dehydration and cramped conditions. But Worsley and Shackleton guided them safely to Elephant Island. They came ashore on 15 April, a narrow, rocky beach being their first solid ground in 497 days. Shortly thereafter, they moved 7 miles (11 km) down the coast to a site they named Cape Wild.

With some of his men beginning to despair, Shackleton decided to fetch help from the whaling stations on South Georgia – 800 nautical miles (1,480 km) away, across a perilous sea on which winds gusted up to 80 mph (130 km/h). In the following days, McNish revamped the largest of the boats, *James Caird*, giving her a second mast, strengthening her hull, and adding decking to protect her interior. Then, on 24 April, Shackleton, Worsley, Crean and McNish sailed away, along with two other crewmembers – Timothy McCarthy and John Vincent – to do the seemingly impossible.

For 16 days they battled through pack ice, freezing gales and heavy seas. On 2 May they were struck by a gigantic wave that almost capsized them. Yet despite rarely being able to take navigational readings, Worsley directed them to South Georgia, where, after a hurricane threatened to smash them against the cliffs, they managed to enter King Haakon Bay on the island's southwest side.

Shackleton decided it was now too dangerous to try to sail to the closest whaling station, so, leaving three men behind, he, Worsley and Crean left to cross an unmapped mountain range to the island's far side. They ascended mountains, crossed glaciers, came down icefalls, and on one occasion they sat on a coiled rope, clung tightly to each other, and shot down a hill at terrifying speed. After travelling for 36 straight hours, they staggered into Stromness station. That night, a ship was sent to pick up the other three men and *James Caird*.

Shackleton next turned his attention to rescuing the men on Elephant Island. A ship at the whaling station tried to reach them, but it was thwarted by heavy ice. Retreating to the Falklands, Shackleton sent out news of his expedition. Two more rescues were attempted before, in August 1916, the Chilean tug *Yelcho* reached Elephant Island. There, Wild had held the party together for 137 days, the 22 men sleeping under the two remaining lifeboats.

Shackleton's last task was to rescue seven members of the Ross Sea Party. In 1915, with 10 men ashore, *Aurora* was trapped in a large floe of ice and borne helplessly away, eventually managing to reach New Zealand. The undersupplied shore party heroically laid all the planned depots, although three of the men died at the end of the effort. The remaining seven were stranded in McMurdo Sound until Shackleton and the relief party finally reached them in January 1917.

**ABOVE:** The landing at Cape Valentine on Elephant Island was difficult, and the prospects unpromising. On the positive side, members of the expedition were able to stand on solid ground for the first time in 16 months.

**RIGHT:** The 22 men who remained on Elephant Island under the command of Wild had to live for four months under two upturned lifeboats set on stone walls 4 feet (1.2 m) high.

**OPPOSITE:** Shackleton, Wild, and the other men during their long wait at Ocean Camp. Maintaining order and hope among his party during the time on the ice was one of Shackleton's greatest achievements.

**TOP:** A busy street in the city of Al-Ḥofuf in eastern Arabia, from where Philby set out on his crossing of the Empty Quarter.

**ABOVE:** An old but massive mud-brick fort. This image was used to illustrate Philby's lecture titled "The Land of Sheba" at the RGS.

# HARRY ST JOHN PHILBY

## EXPLORATION OF ARABIA, 1917–37

HARRY ST JOHN BRIDGER PHILBY (1885–1960) WAS BORN IN CEYLON (NOW SRI LANKA),
BUT AT THE AGE OF 6 HIS MOTHER LEFT HIS FATHER AND TOOK HIM AND HIS THREE
BROTHERS TO LONDON. BRILLIANT, BUT OBSTINATE AND COMBATIVE, YOUNG PHILBY
GAINED A FIRST IN MODERN LANGUAGES AT TRINITY COLLEGE, CAMBRIDGE, FOLLOWING
WHICH HE SPENT A YEAR STUDYING ORIENTAL LANGUAGES.

In 1908 he took a position with the Indian Civil Service in the Punjab. In the ensuing years, he learned Urdu, Punjabi, Baluchi, Persian and Arabic, and in October 1915 his linguistic skills allowed him to join Percy Cox as a civilian administrator with the Mesopotamian Expeditionary Force.

Philby's zeal and intellect saw him appointed as Cox's personal assistant and gain the support of Gertrude Bell. In November 1917, he was sent as the head of a mission to Riyadh to meet with Ibn Saud, the ruler of the Najd (the central region of the Arabian Peninsula). The British were hoping he would renew his war against the al-Rashid of Ha'il, allies of the Ottoman Turks. Philby was immediately drawn to Ibn Saud,

and the two men would maintain a lifelong friendship. When an emissary travelling from Jiddah did not arrive in Riyadh, Philby's superiors claimed that the journey was impossible. To prove them wrong, Philby rode west in December 1917, travelling the 450 miles (720 km) to Taif in 15 days, and proceeding to Jiddah several days later. There he met Sharif Husain, who was being promoted by T.E. Lawrence as the future Arab leader. When Philby tried to convince British officials that it would be better to support Ibn

**BELOW:** The customs house and fort at Aqaba, not long after the city was captured during the First World War.

Saud, he, like William Shakespear before him, was ignored.

In 1918, Ibn Saud agreed to launch an attack on the al-Rashid in return for a subsidy of £5,000 a month. However, he would not allow Philby to accompany him – to avoid the appearance that he was making war on fellow Muslims at the wish of Christians – and instead he provided him with supplies and an escort to explore areas south of Riyadh. In the ensuing weeks, Philby travelled about 300 miles (485 km) southwest along the unmapped Jabal Tuwayq. He then reversed direction and returned via a parallel route.

In the years following the First World War Philby became unhappy with British Middle Eastern policy. He resigned in 1924 but continued to serve as an unofficial advisor to Ibn Saud. For years Philby was keen to become the first European to cross the great desert in southern Arabia known as "the Empty Quarter". Ibn Saud would not support such an expedition, and in 1931 Bertram Thomas beat him to the honour. Crushed, Philby locked himself away for a time, then decided to follow a different route right into the heart of the desert, allowing him to cover a much broader area and carrying out very detailed exploration in the process.

In January 1932, Philby set out with 14 men, 32 camels and food for three months. He zigzagged through conditions so horrific that even the camels suffered from heat and lack of water. He drove his men and animals on, and in March they entered Sulayyil, having travelled almost 1,700 miles (2,700 km) in 90 days. After two days'

**ABOVE**: Philby in Riyadh. In 1939 he stood for the anti-war British People's Party in a by-election for Hythe, Kent. He lost his deposit.

## PHILBY'S LETTER TO HIS WIFE, DORA

While travelling along the border between Saudi Arabia and Yemen on his last major expedition, Philby was fascinated to come across places and people the like of which he had never seen before. From the Wadi Baish, he wrote:

*The garden of Eden must be very like this valley, and the human beings one meets from time to time might have stepped straight out of Genesis, naked except for a loin-cloth and sometimes a rifle ... All prefer walking to riding; none worry about Ramadhan and drink from the brook whenever they are thirsty.*

rest, the party pressed on for another 400 miles (650 km) to fulfil Philby's promise to get to Mecca for the Pilgrimage.

In the ensuing years, Philby made numerous journeys through the Arabian deserts by automobile, once even taking his wife, who became the first European woman to cross Arabia from the Red Sea to the Persian Gulf. His last major expedition came in 1936–37, when Ibn Saud asked him to map the border between Saudi Arabia and Yemen. Starting at Khurma, east of Mecca, he travelled along the boundary between the countries. Near Najran, he made his greatest archaeological contribution: finding rock carvings – "veritable picture galleries of ancient man" – and inscriptions of a pre-Islamic script never seen before in southern Arabia.

Once he reached the coast near Jizan, Philby headed to Khatma. From there he began what he knew would be a brutally difficult journey to Shabwah in Yemen, a city that he believed no European had ever visited. Driven on, despite terrible conditions, he reached Shabwah, only to find that a German photographer had arrived there a few months before.

Philby later converted to Islam, and he lived in Jiddah until he was exiled for criticizing the inefficiency and extravagance of Ibn Saud's successor in 1955. His last years were spent in Lebanon, and he died in Beirut, where he had been staying with his son, the British intelligence officer and Soviet spy Kim Philby.

**BELOW:** The Masjid al-Haram (Sacred Mosque) in Mecca. The largest mosque in the world at 88.2 acres, it surrounds Islam's holiest place, the Kaaba.

# MOUNT EVEREST EXPEDITION, 1924

## BRIGADIER CHARLES BRUCE AND JOHN NOEL

AS EARLY AS 1893, CHARLES GRANVILLE BRUCE OF THE INDIAN ARMY HAD SUGGESTED AN
EXPEDITION TO CLIMB MOUNT EVEREST. THE YEAR BEFORE, AS A LIEUTENANT WITH THE
5TH GURKHA REGIMENT, HE AND FOUR OF HIS MEN HAD JOINED AN EXPEDITION TO THE
KARAKORAM LED BY THE MOUNTAINEER MARTIN CONWAY.

Then in 1893, Bruce accompanied Francis Younghusband on a mission to the Hindu Kush. Everest seemed the next step.

For the next 10 years, Bruce continued to roam the Himalayas, and participated in several major climbing efforts. Finally, in 1920, the government of Tibet granted permission for an attempt to scale Mount Everest from the north. Unable to obtain leave, Bruce could not join the reconnaissance expedition in 1921, so Charles Howard-Bury was appointed leader instead.

During that effort, George Mallory, Edward Wheeler and Guy Bullock became the first men to reach Everest's North Col, at the head of the East Rongbuk Glacier. This was to be the starting point for the planned route the following year: ascending the North Col to the North Ridge and following that and the Northeast Ridge up towards the summit.

Bruce was appointed leader of the next expedition, in 1922. Using yaks as transport animals, Bruce crossed Tibet to the Rongbuk Glacier. From there, 100 Tibetans carried equipment and stores to the initial camps, and 50 Sherpas moved the materials higher up. In late May, George Finch and Geoffrey Bruce – the leader's cousin – reached 27,300 feet (8,321 m) before a failure of the oxygen supply forced a retreat.

The third expedition in 1924 was, like its predecessors, coordinated and funded under the auspices of the Royal Geographical Society (RGS) and the Alpine Club. Bruce was again in charge, with Edward Norton as second-in-command. Others returning from the previous effort were Mallory, the younger Bruce, surgeon Howard Somervell, and John Noel, who was the expedition's photographer and filmmaker. Among the new members was 22-year-old Andrew Irvine.

In March 1924, the expedition entered Tibet from Sikkim, using about 150 Tibetans and 55 Sherpas as porters. Noel took hundreds of pictures and made a remarkable silent film as they

**ABOVE**: For a month, the heavily loaded expedition made its way across Tibet, during which Noel made a valuable record of the lives of the Tibetan people and their interactions with the foreign climbers.

**OPPOSITE**: Camp II, at the East Rongbuk Glacier. Mallory is in the foreground wearing a hat and looking at the camera. Towering above is Mount Kellas, named after Alexander Kellas, who died of a heart attack on the 1921 expedition.

crossed through the remote country. Unfortunately, Charles Bruce had contracted malaria when hunting tigers in India, and while on Tibet's high plain, his health deteriorated, and he had to be evacuated. The leadership passed to Norton.

At the end of April the expedition reached the East Rongbuk Glacier, but a blizzard meant that the first three camps leading to the North Col took about three weeks to erect. As soon as the weather broke, they fixed ropes on the slope to the North Col, and on 21 May, Camp IV was established at about 23,000 feet (7,000 m).

The first summit attempt – by Mallory and Bruce with nine porters – began on 1 June, but four porters turned back without permission, leaving Mallory to establish Camp V at 25,260 feet (7,700 m). The following day three more porters fled, so Mallory and Bruce were forced to retreat without erecting Camp VI, as planned. On their way down, they met Norton and Somervell, already beginning a second attempt.

On 3 June, Norton and Somervell established Camp VI at 26,800 feet (8,170 m). The next morning they started their summit

**ABOVE**: John Noel "kinematographing" an attempted ascent of Mount Everest. Born in Devon, Noel was educated in Switzerland, where he loved the mountains. Posted to India with the army, he became very knowledgeable about the Himalayas.

**BELOW**: The 1924 Everest team. Standing (from left): Irvine, Mallory, Norton, Odell, and John MacDonald. Sitting (from left): Edward Shebbeare, Geoffrey Bruce, Somervell, and Bentley Beetham.

bid, but were forced to rest frequently, as they had not taken supplemental oxygen. After five hours, Somervelle stopped and Norton continued alone, reaching 28,120 feet (8,570 m), a record altitude, before wisely turning around.

On 6 June Mallory set out again from Camp IV, this time in the company of Irvine and plenty of oxygen tanks. The next day they ascended to Camp VI, with Noel Odell and one porter as a support team. On the morning of 8 June Mallory and Irvine began their final ascent, and around 1 p.m., when the mist temporarily cleared, Odell spied them at around 27,950 feet (8,520 m).

Several hours later, after a sudden snowstorm, nothing could be seen of Mallory or Irvine. Odell climbed to Camp VI and waited, but the two men never returned. On 11 June the expedition members began heading down from Camp IV, and four days later, they began the journey home.

Charles Bruce was awarded the Founder's Medal of the RGS the next year. Everest was finally conquered in 1953 by Edmund Hillary and Tenzing Norgay. Mallory's body was discovered in 1999, but whether he and Irvine reached the summit remains unknown.

**ABOVE:** Mallory's hobnail boot, which was discovered with his body at an elevation of about 26,800 feet (8,170 m) in May 1999, 75 years after he and Irvine disappeared.

**BELOW:** Even hidden in the clouds and mist, Mount Everest was still an awesome, and threatening, sight. The lengthy journey to base camp allowed the climbers to acclimatize to the high altitude slowly and safely.

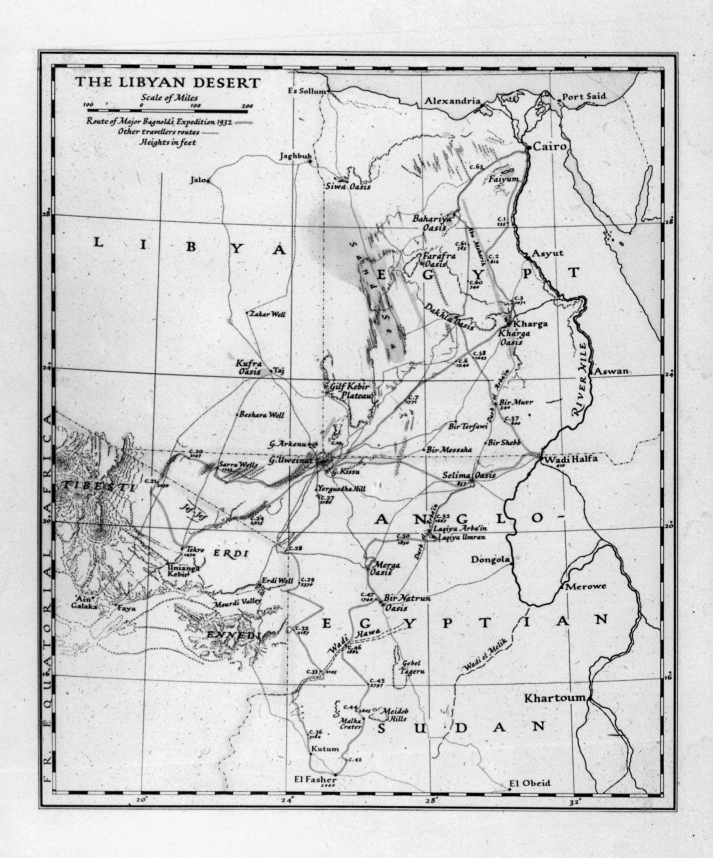

## THE LIBYAN DESERT

*Scale of Miles*

100    0    100    200

*Route of Major Bagnold's Expedition 1932*
*Other travellers routes* ............
*Heights in feet*

Es Sollum
Alexandria
Port Said
Cairo

Jaghbub
C.63
Faiyum

Jalo
Siwa Oasis

L I B Y A
Bahariya Oasis
C.1 *355*

E G Y P T
C.61 *785*
Farafra Oasis
C.2 *612*

Zakar Well
Sand Sea
C.60 *740*
Dakhla Oasis
C.3 *1071*

Kufra Oasis • Taj
Kharga
Kharga Oasis
Aswan

Beshara Well
Gilf Kebir Plateau
C.58 *1445*
C.6 *1240*
Bir Muxr *540*
RIVER NILE

G. Arkenu
C.10
C.7 *1771*
Bir Terfawi
C.57 *600*

C.20 *1147*
Sarra Wells *1735*
G. Uweinat
Bir Messaha
Bir Shebb
Wadi Halfa *410*

TIBESTI
C.21 *2050*
G. Kissu
Selima Oasis *857*

Jef Jef
C.24 *2025*
Yerguedha Hill
C.27 *1180*

A N G L O -

Tekro *1470*
ERDI
C.28
C.52 *1607*
Laqiya Arba'in
Laqiya Umran

Unianga Kebir
C.50 *1850*
Dongola

Ain Galaka • Faya
Erdi Well
C.29 *1370*
Merga Oasis
Merowe

Mourdi Valley
C.47 *1740*
Bir Natrun Oasis

E N N E D I
C.32 *2187*
E G Y P T I A N
Wadi Hawa
C.46 *1882*
Gebel Tageru
Wadi el Melik

C.33 *2105*
C.45 *2797*
Khartoum

C.44 *2605*
Meidob Hills

C.36 *3184*
Malha Crater
S U D A N

Kutum
C.42

El Fasher *1140*
El Obeid

F R · E Q U A T O R I A L · A F R I C A

# RALPH BAGNOLD

## SCIENTIFIC EXPLORATION IN NORTH AFRICA, 1927–38

RALPH ALGER BAGNOLD (1896–1990) MANAGED TO HAVE THREE SEPARATE CAREERS
DURING HIS LIFE – AS A SOLDIER, AN EXPLORER AND A SCIENTIST – AND TO MAKE
SIGNIFICANT CONTRIBUTIONS IN EACH. THE SON OF A COLONEL IN THE ROYAL ENGINEERS
(AND GRANDSON OF A MAJOR-GENERAL IN THE EAST INDIA COMPANY), BAGNOLD
FOLLOWED IN HIS FATHER'S FOOTSTEPS.

Passing out of the Royal Military Academy, Woolwich, in 1915, he joined the School of Military Engineering at Chatham as a second lieutenant in the Royal Engineers. Posted to France shortly thereafter, he fought at the Somme, Ypres and Passchendaele, and was mentioned in dispatches.

After the end of the First World War, the army sent Bagnold, who had reached the rank of captain, to Gonville and Caius College, Cambridge, where he took the engineering tripos. He completed his degree in two years and returned to the army. He joined the 5th Division Signal Company, but on its transfer from the Royal Engineers to the new Royal Corps of Signals, he became an instructor at the Signal Training Centre.

In 1926, Bagnold was posted to Cairo. He had always been interested in the concept of exploring remote parts of the world, and this assignment now gave him the opportunity to engage in desert exploration by motor car. In 1927, he and several friends drove the 350 miles (560 km) from Cairo to the Siwa oasis in the Libyan Desert.

A promotion to major saw Bagnold transferred to the Northwest Frontier of India, where he was in command of the Waziristan Signals. Returning to Egypt while on leave in November 1929, he took a specially modified Model-T Ford from the Farafra oasis

**OPPOSITE:** A map showing the remarkable distances travelled – some 6,000 miles (10,000 km) during Bagnold's 1932–33 expedition.

**BELOW:** Having an automobile along on an expedition did not always make travel as easy as one might hope.

into the midst of the Great Sand Sea and thence to the Ammonite Scarp, a limestone formation with many Cretaceous fossils. Bagnold was back on leave a year later, his party reaching Jebel Uweinat, the mountain at the point where Libya, Egypt and Sudan meet. The return journey took them due east across the desert of northern Sudan, via the Selima oasis.

In 1932, Bagnold and several fellow officers – including Hugh Boustead, who would later command the Sudan Camel Corps – again drove to Jebel Uweinat and made the first ascent of the mountain. From there, they continued on an expedition of 3,700 miles (5,950 km) through the eastern Sahara, exploring parts of Libya, Chad and Sudan. At Jebel Kissu in Sudan they discovered ancient rock paintings. Two years later, Bagnold was awarded the Royal Geographical Society's Founder's Medal.

Reassigned in 1933 as officer commanding signals, China Command, Bagnold was taken ill with what was described as "tropical sprue" and was retired from the army in 1935 as a permanent invalid. It was an assessment that soon proved inaccurate, and he threw himself into researching the physics of blowing sand and the formation of sand dunes. At Imperial College, London, he conducted the first experiments with sand using a wind tunnel. In an attempt to further his knowledge, and under the auspices of the Egyptian Exploration Society, he returned to the Libyan Desert and the Selima Sand Sea in 1938. The party excavated several Neolithic sites and found previously unknown rock art at three different places. In 1941 he published *The Physics of Blown Sand and Desert Dunes*, which is still the standard work on the aeolian movement of sand.

**ABOVE**: A flock of ostriches, taken during Bagnold's expedition of 1932–33 through the eastern Sahara, for which he received the RGS Founder's Medal.

**RIGHT**: Rough going during Bagnold's 1932–33 expedition.

**OPPOSITE**: An ostrich communal nest – called a dump nest. Each egg is about 6 inches (15 cm) long and weighs up to 3 pounds (1.3 kg).

**ABOVE:** The Selima oasis in northern Sudan was a key stopping point on an ancient trade route. It sits on a vast, sandy plain known as the Selima Sandsheet.

**LEFT:** On Bagnold's journey of 1929–30, he discovered some beautiful, but previously little known, artwork on a desert rock face.

**OPPOSITE:** Giant sand ripples at the foot of the Gilf Kebir, a plateau rising about 1,000 feet (300 m) near the southern corner of the Egypt-Libya border.

The start of the Second World War saw Bagnold recalled to the army. Stationed in Cairo, he proposed to General Sir Archibald Wavell that they establish a unit to track enemy movements, harry desert outposts and airfields, and conduct covert patrols behind Italian lines. Bagnold was made a lieutenant-colonel and put in charge of establishing and recruiting what became known as the Long Range Desert Group (LRDG). The force eventually grew to 350 men, many of them New Zealanders and Rhodesians. Among its early leaders were several of Bagnold's friends from his deep desert travels. During the two and a half years of the Desert Campaign, patrols of the LRDG spent all but 15 days behind Axis lines. Bagnold received an OBE for his role in establishing the group.

In 1941 Bagnold relinquished control of the LRDG and was assigned to the general staff in Cairo with the rank of colonel. He was later promoted to brigadier and served as deputy officer-in-chief of signals in the Middle East. His father died in 1943, following which Bagnold was granted a release from further military service and returned to England. There he found that he had been elected a fellow of the Royal Society, a truly remarkable honour for a man who was essentially an amateur scientist.

Several years after the end of the war, Bagnold returned to Imperial College and expanded his research to include the physics of waterborne sand and sediments. Much of his subsequent research – investigating the annual rate at which rivers transport solids – was conducted in collaboration with the U.S. Geological Survey. Bagnold's contributions were recognized by the award of the Wollaston Medal of the Geological Society of London, the Penrose Medal of the Geological Society of America, and the G.K. Warren Prize of the U.S. National Academy of Science, among others.

In the 1970s, Bagnold began to apply his theories to the movement of sand on Mars, and as late as 1978, at the age of 82, he was the keynote speaker at a NASA-sponsored conference on the desert landscapes on Earth and Mars. His last published paper appeared in the *Proceedings of the Royal Society* in 1986, when he was 90 years old.

# FURTHER READING

## BOOKS

Allen, Charles. 2004. *Duel in the Snows: the True Story of the Younghusband Mission to Lhasa*. London: John Murray.

Amundsen, Roald. 1908. *The North-West Passage*. 2 vols. London: John Murray.

Amundsen, Roald. 1912. *The South Pole*. 2 vols. London: John Murray.

Bagnold, Ralph. 1935. *Libyan Sands: Travel in a Dead World*. London: Hodder and Stoughton.

Bagnold, Ralph. 1941. *The Physics of Blown Sand and Desert Dunes*. London: Methuen.

Baker, Samuel White. 1866. *The Albert N'yanza: Great Basin of the Nile*. 2 vols. London: Macmillan.

Ballantine, James. 1866. *The Life of David Roberts*. London: Adam and Charles Black.

Baughman, T.H. 1999. *Pilgrims on the Ice: Robert Falcon Scott's First Antarctic Expedition*. Lincoln, NE, and London: University of Nebraska Press.

Beaglehole, J.C. 1974. *The Life of Captain James Cook*. London: Adam and Charles Black.

Bell, Gertrude. 1911. *Amurath to Amurath*. London: William Heinemann.

Bird, Isabella. 1879. *A Lady's Life in the Rocky Mountains*. New York: G.P. Putnam's Sons.

Bishop, Isabella Bird. 1899. *The Yangtze Valley and Beyond*. London: John Murray.

Bomann-Larsen, Tor. 2006. *Roald Amundsen*. Stroud, UK: Sutton Publishing.

Browne, Janet. 1995. *Charles Darwin, Vol. 1: Voyaging*. London: Jonathan Cape.

Buisseret, David (editor). 2007. *The Oxford Companion to World Exploration*. 2 vols. Oxford: Oxford University Press.

Burton, Richard Francis. 1860. *The Lake Regions of Central Africa*. 2 vols. London: Longmans.

Crane, David. 2005. *Scott of the Antarctic*. London: HarperCollins.

Darwin, Charles. 1905. *The Voyage of the Beagle*. London: John Murray.

Dunmore, John. 1965–69. *French Explorers in the Pacific*. 2 vols. Oxford: Clarendon Press.

FitzRoy, Robert. 1839. *Narrative of the Surveying Voyages of His Majesty's Ships Adventure and Beagle*. 4 vols. London: Henry Colburn.

Fleming, Fergus. 1998. *Barrow's Boys*. London: Granta Books.

Graham, Ian. 2002. *Alfred Maudslay and the Maya: a Biography*. London: British Museum Press.

Grant, James Augustus. 1864. *A Walk Across Africa*. Edinburgh: William Blackwood and Sons.

Gurney, Alan. 2000. *The Race to the White Continent*. New York and London: W.W. Norton.

Hedin, Sven. 1926. *My Life as an Explorer*. London: Cassell.

Helferich, Gerard. 2004. *Humboldt's Cosmos: Alexander von Humboldt and the Latin American Journey that Changed the World*. New York: Gotham Books.

Hopkirk, Peter. 1980. *Foreign Devils on the Silk Road*. London: John Murray.

Hopkirk, Peter. 1990. *The Great Game*. London: John Murray.

Howell, Georgina. 2006. *Daughter of the Desert: the Remarkable Life of Gertrude Bell*. London: Macmillan.

Howgego, Raymond John. 2003. *Encyclopedia of Exploration to 1800*. Sydney: Hordern House.

Howgego, Raymond John. 2004. *Encyclopedia of Exploration 1800 to 1850*. Sydney: Hordern House.

Howgego, Raymond John. 2006. *Encyclopedia of Exploration 1850 to 1940: the Oceans, Islands, and Polar Regions*. Sydney: Hordern House.

Howgego, Raymond John. 2008. *Encyclopedia of Exploration 1850 to 1940: Continental Exploration*. Sydney: Hordern House.

Huntford, Roland. 1979. *Scott and Amundsen*. London: Hodder and Stoughton.

Huntford, Roland. 1985. *Shackleton*. London: Hodder and Stoughton.

Huntford, Roland. 1997. *Nansen: the Explorer as Hero*. London: Duckworth.

Jeal, Tim. 1973. *Livingstone*. London: William Heinemann.

Jeal, Tim. 2007. *Stanley*. London: Faber and Faber.

Jeal, Tim. 2011. *Explorers of the Nile*. London: Faber and Faber.

Johnston, Harry H. 1923. *The Story of My Life*. Indianapolis: Bobbs-Merrill Company.

Keay, John (editor). 1991. *The Royal Geographical Society History of World Exploration*. London: Hamlyn.

Livingstone, David, and Charles Livingstone. 1865. *Narrative of an Expedition to the Zambesi*. London: John Murray.

Maitland, Alexander. 1971. *Speke*. London: Constable.

Markham, Albert Hastings. 1878. *The Great Frozen Sea*. London: Dalby, Isbister.

McGregor, Alasdair. 2004. *Frank Hurley: a Photographer's Life*. Camberwell, Victoria: Viking.

Middleton, Dorothy. 1949. *Baker of the Nile*. London: Falcon Press.

Monroe, Elizabeth. 1973. *Philby of Arabia*. London: Faber and Faber.

Moorehead, Alan. 1960. *The White Nile*. London: Hamish Hamilton.

Murray, W.H. 1953. *The Story of Everest, 1921–1952*. London: J.M. Dent & Sons.

Nansen, Fridtjof. 1890. *The First Crossing of Greenland*. 2 vols. London: Longmans, Green.

Nansen, Fridtjof. 1897. *Farthest North*. 2 vols. Westminster: Archibald Constable.

Nares, George Strong. 1878. *Narrative of a Voyage to the Polar Sea*. 2 vols. London: Sampson Low Marston, Searle & Rivington.

Oulié, Marthe. 1938. *Charcot of the Antarctic*. London: John Murray.

Pakenham, Thomas. 1991. *The Scramble for Africa*. London: Weidenfeld & Nicolson.

Palmquist, Peter E. 1983. *Carleton Watkins: Photographer of the American West*. Albuquerque: University of New Mexico Press.

Philby, Harry St John. 1948. *Arabia Days: an Autobiography*. London: Robert Hale.

Quartermain, L.B. 1967. *South to the Pole*. London: Oxford University Press.

Riffenburgh, Beau. 1993. *The Myth of the Explorer*. London: Belhaven Press.

Riffenburgh, Beau. 2004. *Nimrod*. London and New York: Bloomsbury.

Schlagintweit, Herman, Robert Schlagintweit, and Adolf Schlagintweit. 1861–66. *Results of a Scientific Mission to India and High Asia*. 4 vols. London: F.A. Brockhaus.

Scott, Robert Falcon. 1913. *Scott's Last Expedition*. 2 vols. London: Smith, Elder & Company.

Shackleton, Ernest. 1919. *South*. London: William Heinemann.

Speke, John Hanning. 1863. *Journal of the Discovery of the Source of the Nile*. London: William Blackwood and Sons.

Stein, M. Aurel. 1903. *Sand-Buried Ruins of Khotan*. London: Hurst and Blackett.

Walker, Annabel. 1995. *Aurel Stein: Pioneer of the Silk Road*. London: John Murray.

Wallis, John Peter Richard. 1941. *Thomas Baines of King's Lynn: Explorer and Artist*. London: Jonathan Cape.

Winstone, H.V.F. 1976. *Captain Shakespear*. London: Jonathan Cape.

Yelverton, David. 2000. *Antarctica Unveiled: Scott's First Expedition and the Quest for the Unknown Continent*. Boulder, CO: University Press of Colorado.

# WEB SITES

Bell, Gertrude — www.gerty.ncl.ac.uk

Dumont d'Urville, J.S.C. — www.teara.govt.nz/en/biographies/1d19/dumont-durville-jules-sebastien-cesar

Fram Museum (Nansen & Amundsen) — www.frammuseum.no

Livingstone, David — www.westminster-abbey.org/our-history/people/david-livingstone

Maudslay, Alfred — http://www.mexicolore.co.uk/maya/home/the-life-of-alfred-maudslay

Royal Geographical Society — www.rgs.org

Schlagintweit Brothers — www.schlagintweit.de

Scott Polar Research Institute — www.spri.cam.ac.uk

Shakespear, William — http://britishlibrary.typepad.co.uk/untoldlives/2015/01/the-death-of-a-political-agent-captain-shakespear.html

Stein, Marc Aurel — www.siraurelstein.org.uk

Watkins, Carleton — www.carletonwatkins.org

# INDEX

Page numbers in *italic* type refer to
pictures or their captions.

**ABOVE**: Europeans and a Damara - carrying a lamp - walking beside a covered wagon at night in southern Africa, as a comet crosses the sky in the distance. Watercolour by Thomas Baines, 1862.